"Some people write about nice concepts. Some people live those truths and then happen to write about them. Terry, thanks for leading the way with your life first. Both your life and words have greatly impacted my family and me."

—HIP WADERS, friend and counsel (chapter 10)

"I met Terry a few years ago after a bike purchase my wife made for me on Father's Day. Cheryl, my wife of thirty-eight years, was my whole life, my treasure. A year ago, she left this world unexpectedly. I fell into unimaginable grief. The surprise friendship my wife started me on with Terry continues on the bike as God tries to heal my broken heart. I have a lot of miles to go. Terry encourages us all to be the surprise . . . like he has been in my life."

—GARY, friend and fellow "separated-at-birth" cycle-o-holic (chapter 22)

"Oh Terry. It's taken me a few days to absorb this book thing. Me—in a book? Crazy! Sometimes I still can't believe God takes simple me with a simple job and makes my life into something simply beautiful. I love my job and I love all the wonderful people I get to serve—it's so much fun. And Terry, I do love you."

—WILMA, The seventy-something busser at D'Amico Cucina in Wayzata (chapter 3)

"I've been waiting for Terry's "God" since my childhood—which included twelve years of perfect attendance in Sunday school. I can still hear my mother, Bette, on Sunday morning barking, "Wwwake up! You're going to church no matter how hungover you are!" Fifty years later I "wake up!" Just in the nick of time. And am I ever Surprised."

—TOOKIE, friend, future million-seller author (chapters 21, 25, and 30)

"Terry and Mary make friends effortlessly. I think that's because they truly love people. When Jesus said, 'Love your neighbor as yourself,' I suspect this is pretty close to what he had in mind. I'm proud of you, son. I bet the Father is too."

—GILBERT ESAU, Terry's dad and Mary's father-in-law (chapter 16)

"In a culture preoccupied with bringing people to God, Terry Esau's refreshing views of a loving God actually loose among us seem far more interested in bringing God to people. If God is indeed ringing out across the nations, calling people back to authenticity, to real relationship with Him, maybe, just maybe, He's using the Terry Esaus of this world as His Church bells."

—RICK BARRON, musician, singer, friend (chapters 28 and 29)

"Terry doesn't see me the same way that I see myself. His gift for kindness has reached new heights in his exaggeration of the stature of The Garlington Northern. It is not just false modesty, nor my qu[...]
compels me to set the record straight, it is in fa[...]

D1397448

shortcomings that I feel the need to address. I am only six foot two."

—TOM, aka The Garlington Northern, friend and favorite draft (chapter 24)

"Sometimes people ask me, 'As Terry's wife, do you feel pressured into going along with these "experiments"'? Yes I do! But really, I never would have wanted to miss out on this journey because it has been so gratifying to see lives impacted and changed."

—MARY ESAU, BFF and wife (chapter—the whole book)

"A special author, a special soul, who's been given the gift of bringing spiritual significance to the real moments of life—moments that change real people's lives forever. He brought one of those moments to our lives, and nothing has been the same. Terry has inspired us; he is fulfilling a destiny."

—TYLER AND MARISSA, brand-new friends (chapter 37)

"Terry continues to take extremely difficult ideas and moments in life and present them in ways that are approachable. This book will inspire you to hold the balance of being the incarnate Christ, or 'The Surpris-ee' for others while continuing to see all God's 'surprises' in your own life. His stories and experiences will not only make you laugh, but will give you vivid, mental pictures of how we are to love people and, as a result, love God."

—JEN LAKE, widow of Kyle Lake, late pastor of UBC, Waco, Texas (chapter 20)

"*Be the Surprise* is delightful! Terry Esau's best work ever! *Be the Surprise* is a captivating and an invigorating motivation to not live quietly with your faith in God, but rather to find the excitement in playing the leading role in your own life and community as one of God's *greatest miracles! It is brilliant spiritual sustenance for the everyday soul!*"

—HEIDI ROSATI, friend, lover-of-people, and president of Retro (chapter 37)

"*Be the Surprise* by Terry Esau opened my heart and mind into everyday moments to live and share God's love. Gazing at stars and staring at the cross deepens my daily walk in faith. Wow—how exciting to realize that God is always with me and ready to help me be a surprise with His love."

—PADDLE, stogie-smokin' friend (chapters 10 and 31)

"Yeah, we mowed grass together for a lot of years. He treated me pretty good, that Esau fella. Fairly regular oil changes. Sharpened my blade . . . occasionally. I'm not sure how many years I've got left, but as long as my 'teeth' are still good, he and I will be cutting the fescue."

—YARDIE, Terry's Yardman riding mower (chapters 12 and 15)

"Woof, woof, ruff——ru, ru, ruff!" (Literal translation: I like him pretty a lot cuz he feed me and take me pee when I got to pee—and sometimes poop. Don't like to baths. Bacon real much yummy.)

—BAILEY, Terry's Springer Spaniel (chapter 32)

BE THE SURPRISE

EXPERIMENTS IN SPONTANEOUS FAITH

TERRY
ESAU

OUR GUARANTEE TO YOU

We believe so strongly in the message of our books that we are making this quality guarantee to you. If for any reason you are disappointed with the content of this book, return the title page to us with your name and address and we will refund to you the list price of the book. To help us serve you better, please briefly describe why you were disappointed. Mail your refund request to: NavPress, P.O. Box 35002, Colorado Springs, CO 80935.

For a free catalog
of NavPress books & Bible studies call
1-800-366-7788 (USA) or 1-800-839-4769 (Canada).

www.navpress.com

The Navigators is an international Christian organization. Our mission is to advance the gospel of Jesus and His kingdom into the nations through spiritual generations of laborers living and discipling among the lost. We see a vital movement of the gospel, fueled by prevailing prayer, flowing freely through relational networks and out into the nations where workers for the kingdom are next door to everywhere.

NavPress is the publishing ministry of The Navigators. The mission of NavPress is to reach, disciple, and equip people to know Christ and make Him known by publishing life-related materials that are biblically rooted and culturally relevant. Our vision is to stimulate spiritual transformation through every product we publish.

ISBN-13: 978-1-60006-196-7
ISBN-10: 1-60006-196-6

Cover design by The DesignWorks Group, Jason Gabbert
Cover image by Steve Gardner, PixelWorks Studio
Creative Team: Kris Wallen, Liz Heaney, Darla Hightower, Arvid Wallen, Kathy Guist

Some of the anecdotal illustrations in this book are true to life and are included with the permission of the persons involved. All other illustrations are composites of real situations, and any resemblance to people living or dead is coincidental.

Unless otherwise identified, all Scripture quotations in this publication are taken from the *THE MESSAGE* (MSG). Copyright © 1993, 1994, 1995, 1996, 2000, 2001, 2002, 2005. Used by permission of NavPress Publishing Group; Other versions used include: the *New American Standard Bible* (NASB), © The Lockman Foundation 1960, 1962, 1963, 1968, 1971, 1972, 1973, 1975, 1977, 1995; and the HOLY BIBLE: NEW INTERNATIONAL VERSION® (NIV®), Copyright © 1973, 1978, 1984 by International Bible Society, used by permission of Zondervan Publishing House, all rights reserved.

Library of Congress Cataloging-in-Publication Data
Esau, Terry, 1954-
  Be the surprise : experiments in spontaneous faith / Terry Esau.
     p. cm.
  Includes bibliographical references.
  ISBN-13: 978-1-60006-196-7
  ISBN-10: 1-60006-196-6
  1. Christian life. 2. Spirituality. I. Title.
BV4501.3.E826 2008
248.4--dc22
                          2007032449

Printed in the United States of America

1 2 3 4 5 6 7 8 / 12 11 10 09 08

To my dad,
Who seems taller as he gets older.
Who seems wiser as I get older.
I love you, Dad.

CONTENTS

ACKNOWLEDGMENTS

I've got a killer family. From Mary, down through the girls, to my son-in-law, and on out to the fringes of the Esaus and Soholts. Some are more fringe than others, but they're all part of the crockpot stew that functions as my home base. I love being in the mix of life with you all.

Experiences and relationships — I'm a big fan of both. Most of the stories in this book have been unconsciously cowritten on the pages of my life by the people that I call friends. You, my friends, are my greatest assets. Know that I love you and am eternally grateful for you. I especially want to thank those whose stories are told in these pages — thanks for letting me share a bit of you with my readers.

Liz Heaney, my editor — thanks for giving me the ten-bushel discount on content corrections and grammatical tweaks. Thanks for helping me say what I wanted to say.

To all my friends at NavPress — thanks for continuing to believe in me and for offering a platform for my ramblings.

Thanks to my carbon fiber therapist (my bicycle) who has yet to speak a word to me.

And to the Composer of surprises who has written an

increasingly nonlinear score for me to play. I may not be playing it perfectly, but I'm sure having fun making noise.

1

FORTUNES IN MY COOKIE

I ate at Chin's Asia Fresh today. My fortune said:

If you continually give, you will continually receive.

It's weird. I've begun exploring the process of *Being* the Surprise, but I keep ending up on the *receiving* end. I keep intending to give, but I keep getting.

Makes me wonder if giving and receiving are conjoined twins. After all, they're attached to each other, share a common heart. What benefits one benefits the other. When one person gives something, another person always gets something, so if everyone were giving, everyone would be getting. Nongetters wouldn't exist. There'd be no category for those without: there'd be no "get-less" people.

Funny thing is, we can't choose to get; we can only choose to give. If we choose to be givers, we have the potential to create a tidal wave that would turn the whole world into a sea of receivers. Giving has that kind of power. We just have to start giving, and then two weeks later, when the pyramid scheme kicks in, we'll get 100,000 one-dollar bills in our mailbox and . . . sorry, oops, I slipped into an Amway warp.

Seriously, I'm no health-and-wealth/name-it-and-claim-it dude, but if the world someday, somehow, were to understand the power of giving, we'd all, and I mean *all*, have plenty.

If you continually give, you will continually receive.

But the opposite is also true. If you continually receive, you will continually give. At least this has been true for me.

A few years ago I conducted an experiment that has resuscitated my awareness that God has wrapped himself around the moments of my days — that he is actively involved in my activities, present with, in, and through me. This awareness has left me glazed in gratitude, coated in awe and thankfulness that this amazing God would choose me to ride sidekick with him through his days, my days — our days.

Yeah, that's me, the guy with the goofy grin in the passenger seat.

Now that I have this renewed awareness, I want to glaze someone else's life. I want to give back, to Be the Surprise for others. I want to honor the one who gave to me and to become a giver at heart.

I want to go beyond being the *surprise-ee* to becoming the *surprise-or*.

But I'm getting ahead of you. Let me back up and tell you how all this surprise stuff started.

A few years ago a film director contacted me, saying he

wanted to take a story from my first book, *Blue Collar God/ White Collar God*, and make it into a movie. He flew to Minneapolis and we spent a weekend working out the details. He told me, "Everyone needs a rich grandmother, and I want to be yours." Cool. The guy had a prominent 5 o'clock shadow, so my imagination had to work overtime to see him as Sweet Little Granny Moneybags, but I was willing to give it my best effort. We shook hands and he got on his plane and flew back to la-la land.

That was the last I heard from him. Moneybags evidently got fired and no one else in the company cared diddly about my project. He and the project both disappeared. For good.

I was bummed. How could this have happened? It seemed so certain, like such a God thing. (Note to self: There's a good chance I might be a fallible predictor of God things. Or more accurately, "my things" aren't necessarily "God things.")

I sat down in front of the TV, like any good, depressed American male would do, and started flipping channels. I stopped when I got to *Fear Factor*. As I watched the show, I started wondering, *What is the fascination with reality TV? Is it that we seem to be eavesdropping on something raw, real, alive? Have we inadvertently stumbled upon a spontaneous, unscripted adventure? . . .* And that got me imagining episodes for a reality spirituality TV show called *The God Factor*.

> **Host:** It's time for the Rapture Round, the prayer competition where one contestant will prove to be more righteously sanctimonious than the others and earn the right to wear the "hallelujah halo." Billy Bob, we'll start with

you. Please pray a prayer using the words *Birkenstocks, pumpernickel, tweezers,* and *Red Bull.*

Billy Bob: *(Drops emphatically to knees.)* Our most gracious God and Father, pluck the sin from my heart with your <u>tweezers</u> of righteousness . . . and multiply your blessings to feed my soul as you did with the two fishes and five loaves of <u>pumpernickel</u>. Wean me from the cheap, tawdry thirst for earthly pleasures and quench my spirit with the <u>Red Bull</u> of spiritual contentment. All this I pray in the name of the Father, the Son, and the Holy Spirit, who doesn't wear any high-falutin', mass-market sandals, but if he did, he'd slide his holy heels into a pair of . . . <u>Birkenstocks!</u> Amen.

I quickly threw out the idea for a TV show, but I liked the reality part, so I opted for an experiment. I decided to pray three words for thirty days:

Surprise me, God.

No list, no agenda. I wanted to request *his* list and *his* agenda, to invite God to bring into my life whatever he wants, without reservation.

Then I purposed to write down everything that happened — everything. Who I talked with, what we talked about, what I thought about what we talked about. I decided to keep a record of every movie I saw, every book I read, and what I thought about them.

At this point I started wondering, *Is this a biblical concept? Does God even like to surprise people?* So I did a quick mental run-through of the Bible.

Adam. One morning Adam wakes up with a side ache. He rubs open his eyes and sees the most beautiful creature he has ever seen — Eve. I picture God peeking around a tree ten yards away whispering, "Surprise."

Noah. "Build a ship where?"

"Right here is good. It's, uh, gonna rain."

"Shipworthy rain?"

"Yup."

"Excuse me, but did you say two of *every* animal?"

Jonah. "Here fishy, fishy, fishy . . ."

Daniel. This is the story I like the best. Personally, I don't think Daniel was the one surprised that day — I think it was the lions. Picture this. A human gets dumped into a den of carnivores fresh off a forced fast. Minutes earlier they had been licking their paws in anticipation. Now, they look at each other, then look at the ground, and wander into their respective corners mumbling something about not being hungry, not being in the mood to rip Dan limb from limb. I imagine one of the lions curling up into a fetal position, crying, "Who am I?" (This was the very first identity crisis in the history of lions.)

Mary. "You will give birth to the son of God . . . without any, uh, you know."

Jesus and the Resurrection. Not many people saw that one coming.

So, I concluded — yes, God does like to surprise people.

Then I pulled out 1 Corinthians 2:9: "No eye has seen, no ear has heard, no mind has conceived what God has prepared for those who love him" (1 Corinthians 2:9, NIV).

Or as Eugene Peterson puts it in *The Message*, "No one's ever seen or heard anything like this, never so much as imagined anything quite like it — what God has arranged for those who love him." In other words, God has some stuff up his sleeve for us that will shock our socks off. Surprise!

So, I did my 30-Day Surprise Me experiment.[1] And it was a blast. In fact, I kept doing it for two years.

But then I realized I was developing a spiritual paunch. I was becoming a professional observer of God's activity in my life, a spiritual spectator. Not a bad way to spend your days, but it wasn't enough. I began to realize I was missing the full potential of what God intended.

When the Pharisees questioned Jesus as to which law was the greatest, he said, "Love the Lord your God with all your passion and prayer and intelligence" (Matthew 22:37). But Jesus didn't stop there. He went on to say, "Oh, one more thing, fellas, love others as well as you love yourself."

If I never choose to *engage* with God in what he is doing in the world, then I'm missing the second half of Jesus' command — the neighbor part. I've pulled out of the curve before completing the circle.

This is where this book comes in. If *Surprise Me* is about spiritual inhaling, then *Be the Surprise* is about spiritually exhaling. If *Surprise Me* is about recognizing what God is up to in my life, then *Be the Surprise* is me saying to God, "Now that I see what you're doing in my life, please God, let me be a part of it. Let me play the role that you have for me *in that* activity. I don't want to miss out on the fun. Let me go beyond being the surprise-ee to becoming the surprise-or. I want to love my neighbor as myself, in tangible ways."

I've found that God's generosity is like a leaky faucet. Just as I can't stop my leaky faucets at home (without two hundred bucks and a call to my plumber), I can't stop God's graciousness either. He has an ocean of grace above me. He gives, and gives, and gives.

He's a "philanthrop-aholic."

Constant receiving creates saturation. That fullness ought to produce a desire to give to others. Because God generously surprises us, we naturally want to Be the Surprise for others.

Remember when you were a little kid and you'd go outside during a rain shower, crank your head back, stick out your tongue, and joyfully catch the raindrops? That's us. We do the same thing when it comes to God's grace. We're grace catchers.

So look up. Catch. Receive.

And out of your fullness, give.

BLOOD SUCKER OR BLOOD GIVER?

You'll never guess my very first action in this be-the-hands-of-Jesus experiment. I smashed one of his creatures. Yep, you read that right. I was sitting in my car, praying, *God, let me Be the Surprise,* when I heard the buzzing of a mosquito. "Surprise, you little . . . !" *THWAP!* I slapped that little blood-sucker into the afterlife. Purgatory-ized him.

Be the Surprise was under way!

I wiped the juicy carcass of that pest on my pant leg, started the car, and headed toward my first meeting of the day.

As I was driving, I had this thought . . .

Mosquitoes *take* blood.

At the Bloodmobile you *give* blood.

I've done both.

Mosquitoes don't cause initial pain; the discomfort comes later. At the Bloodmobile you feel the initial prick, but later you get a cookie.

The moral of this story?

Cookies don't itch.

Sooner or later you're going to lose some blood. It's inevitable. Sooner or later life will get uncomfortable — a prick now, an itch later.

May as well choose to be a giver.

INCOGNITO PHILANTHROPY

I've been Wilma-tized.

Most people don't notice her. She's not tall, she's not young, she's not loud. She wears a nondescript brown smock. She doesn't swagger, doesn't schmooze, doesn't intrude.

Wilma is a seventy-four-year-old busser. She schleps dishes at D'Amico Cucina, a little Italian restaurant near my house, and has been cleaning up messes for as long as I can remember.

Last week I was at D'Amico's meeting a friend, Booker, for lunch. When Wilma walked by our table, Booker said, "I know that woman. She was my lunchroom lady in junior high."

I said, "Wilma?"

"I don't know her name, but that's her all right."

Through the course of our lunch, I was telling Booker about my desire to Be the Surprise, to be a good neighbor, a servant.

Wilma came by again and I stopped her. "Do you know who this guy is, Wilma?"

"Well he looks familiar, but I . . . don't know."

Booker said, "You were my lunch lady in junior high. You served me lunch a bunch of years ago when I was a snot-nosed punk. Thanks."

"Oh . . . well. So nice to see you again," Wilma blushed, and went about her business.

Wilma doesn't handle compliments well. I don't think she's used to them. She's probably never fished for one in her life. It's not that she wouldn't or doesn't appreciate praise, it's just not in her nature to throw in the line.

It's in her nature to give.

When I look at Wilma, I see Mother Teresa up to her elbows in dishes. I see the Bill Gates Foundation of Covert Benevolence. Wilma has banked kindness for years, and she quietly empties the account every day. She goes from table to table, doling out unpretentious smiles like spoonfuls of sugar, casually resting her hand on weary shoulders.

I'm not sure Wilma knows the good she is doing, which makes the good she does that much more penetrating.

As she walked away from Booker and me, a lightbulb went on over my head. *Whoa. Wilma. She lives what I'm talking about. She's the ultimate servant because she doesn't even know she is one. I need to talk with her.*

The next time she came by our table, I said, "Wilma, may I interview you sometime?"

"Oh, Terry, I'm not looking for another job. I love this one. In fact, this will most likely be my last job."

"No, I don't want to hire you. I want to interview you for a book I'm writing."

You should have seen the look she gave me. She sprouted a crooked grin, grabbed a few dishes from our table, and took off.

When I went home, I started wondering how Wilma became such a servant at heart. She doesn't seem to have an agenda, nor does she give in order to get something for herself. How did she become an incognito philanthropist?

We've all seen the well-bankrolled celebrities who donate 10K to some charity and then hold a press conference to announce it. Plenty of foundations showcase the name of their founders. We've seen building after building with a name engraved on a brick in the lobby, letting everyone know that William Buford Thoroughgood IV made the edifice possible. Little brass nameplates on pews and stickers in hymnals, all saying, "Ain't I something?"

But Wilma? Wilma wears a brown smock.

Hoping to tap into the motivation for her gracious spirit, I coerced her into an interview at Starbucks a week later. She told me she comes from a large family with Depression-era values and a stripped-down, raw faith. She has no desires in life, other than to live and love God and people. "You can't *do* good without *being* good. And God is the good in me." Wilma didn't say that out loud, but that's what I heard in her story. She knows the God of good. She has lived inside him for a lifetime, and he lives inside of her.

She went on to tell me about Brenda, a regular diner at D'Amico's. Wilma had bussed Brenda's dishes for years. Always said "hi," asked about her kids, her life. The two became friends.

When her mom died, where did Brenda turn to for help to

deal with it? When she needed someone to hold her up, who did she run to? Not her priest. Not her pastor. Not her counselor. When this woman needed help, she came looking for Wilma, her busser.

As it turns out, robes, ties, or psychological degrees dispense love no better than a simple brown smock. When our lives get broken, we go to the one who knows us, loves us, and cares for us. If that's our busser, then that's exactly who we want to be with.

By the end of our interview, I realized something: Wilma's true value isn't in the good she *does*, but in the good she *is*. Her God is good, and since she has spent a lifetime ingesting him, he oozes out of her pores, naturally, unconsciously, purely.

That's why doing good is not a conscious act for her. Who Wilma is, is what she does. Who she has followed, is how she leads. Who she has loved, is how she loves.

Before I left Starbucks that day, Wilma put her hand on my shoulder and told me she loves me. My busser loves me.

Wilma is a servant, the highest rung on the upside-down ladder. She loves people, and to keep busy while she's doing that, she busses tables. And she couldn't be happier.

THE SEED CRACKED OPEN

By Hafiz

It used to be
That when I would wake in the morning
I could with confidence say,
"What am I going to do?"

That was before the seed
Cracked open.

. . . .

Now when I awake
All the internal instruments play the same music:

"God, what love-mischief can we do

For the world

Today?"

KISSING TOO HARD

I pulled up to Caribou Coffee to meet with two pastors from a church in Eden Prairie. They were planning to do the Surprise Me experiment with their church — toddlers through AARPers. As we were talking, one of them had an unchecked flashback and told us a weird story from his college days.

One night he took a girl he'd been dating to the France Avenue Drive-In Theater. We all know what happens at drive-in theaters — the seat gets reclined, you yawn and stretch so that your arm casually falls around your girlfriend's shoulder, you turn down the audio from the movie, and . . .

Well, our future pastor — this dispenser of the Word of God who would one day down the road be doing premarital counseling — started making out with this girl. (I know, I thought these religious types had kissed dating good-bye.)

But the thrill was gone in about thirty seconds.

As he told it, either this girl was a terribly inexperienced kisser, or she had significant technique and embouchure issues. Either way, he told us, "It was painful!" She kissed too hard. Passion is good, but jackhammer mashing? Not so much.

All of a sudden someone from the car behind came up and

rapped on the window. According to him, this normally would have been an imposition, but at the moment it was salvation. The redemption of his lips.

Relieved, he readily rolled down the window and asked what his savior wanted. The woman said, "What do *you* want, buddy? You keep flashing your brake lights at us. KNOCK IT OFF!"

Our holy man of the cloth said he thought maybe he'd been slamming his foot on the brake because he was subconsciously trying to STOP the pain.

The other pastor lightheartedly threw out, "That's love, baby."

"It sure didn't *feel* like love."

After I stopped laughing, I immediately had this strange mental flash. Here's what I thought.

We Christians kiss too hard. We try to evangelize people. We throw truth at them like 96-mph fastballs. We throw it right down the plate of their heart and are almost pleased when they swing and miss. "What . . . you can't handle the truth?"

We judge, we protest, we boycott, we chastise, we humiliate, we divide, we demean, we exacerbate, we excoriate.

We kiss too hard!

Whatever happened to love? To holding hands, an arm around the shoulder? A kiss on the cheek? A simple smile? Jesus said, "Love your neighbor as yourself" (Matthew 22:39, NIV). He didn't say evangelize your neighbor as yourself.

Love is the opener.

Love opens hearts. Not truth. Not condemnation. Not even evangelism.

Love.

If we don't have love, we have no right to evangelize — we have nothing *to* evangelize.

The whole world is feeling for its brakes, trying to relieve the pressure of religion's abrasive advances. People just want to make it stop because "it doesn't feel like love." So let's back off, take a breath, put our arm around our neighbor, and start over.

If Be the Surprise is anything other than an act of love, it's a selfish, unwelcome kiss that will do more harm than good. It's stolen, not given. And there will be no second date.

6

A CHORAL CHRIST*MISS*

The Esau family carolers are a choral train that's a semitone or two away from derailment. Our choir, and I use that term loosely, ranges from ten-year-old Davis to my eighty-seven-year-old dad. We've got more basses than sopranos, more fortissimo than finesse, and more pizzazz than pitch.

Tonight's predominantly hard-of-hearing audience thinks we're the Midwestern branch of the Mormon Tabernacle Choir, even though we often come in parkas and snow boots. They even think my dad is Mel Tormé, a.k.a. The Velvet Fog. Our music is all memorized — or should I say that we are singing *from* memory, which isn't the same thing at all. The notes and words are relative — like us — sibling harmony, niece and nephew libretto.

That being said, we are the longest-running Christmas day show ever at the Good Samaritan Nursing Home in Mountain Lake, Minnesota. We have warbled our Christmas carol repertoire for a good twenty-five years, consecutively. Five of us kids, spouses, sixteen grandkids, a few spouses of grandkids, and Mom and Dad. If the Good Samaritan were a Broadway theater, we would all be up for lifetime achievement awards, not to mention a few Tony's.

Every year, on Christmas night, right before we open presents, we pile into six or so cars and drive the four blocks to the Good Sam. We review our set list as we are walking in, and by the time we hit the first wing, our show is prepped, loaded, and staged. Dad gives the note and the crooning begins.

Halfway through "Joy to the World," the hallways start filling up with people in wheelchairs and walkers. Some of the residents sing along, some smile, and some turn up their televisions so they can hear Pat Sajak over our apparently annoying festivity. We do four or five songs in each corridor of the building. Then we usually pop our heads into doorways and wish people a Merry Christmas.

Dad knows most of the residents. He's older than most of them. He puts his arm around shoulders and smiles a sonorous holiday greeting, then herds us to the next wing of the building.

A couple of years ago someone asked my kids what their favorite childhood memory of Christmas was. Taylor, the youngest, said it was caroling at the Good Sam, seeing the smiles on the faces of those people.

Our little caroling tradition began as a way to give back, to help dissolve some loneliness on a night when no one should be lonely. It was our family's way of Being the Surprise at Christmas. It has been one of the best, most rewarding traditions my parents ever initiated. They won't be around too many more years, but the rest of us hope to keep this tradition going far beyond them.

This past Christmas we added a twist to our show. We arrived a little earlier than usual. All the residents were still in the dining room having dinner, so we decided to be the dinner music. As we walked into the dining hall, we noticed a piano. Now, you need to know that my oldest sister, Dianne, is a killer pianist. You name it, she can play it — and not just play it, she makes whoever she is accompanying sound amazing. I knew as soon as I saw the piano that this was our chance to put on a presentable concert.

And we did . . . *she* did. We brought the house down . . . well, it's a nursing home so it was a restrained exuberance, but I'm almost certain that if the residents were allowed to carry cigarette lighters, we would certainly have been coaxed into an encore.

Halfway through our show, I said, "Dianne, do a solo!" She fought it until she realized she didn't have a choice.

As Dianne played, I watched her bring smiles and cheer to people — including us, her family. My sister was using her gift, and giving it for all of us to enjoy, but she was also giving us something deeper. She was giving us herself. *She* was the gift. We think the gift is the talent or the act of kindness, but the *person* is the gift. Talent or kindness is just the visible expression of that gift.

When we decide to Be the Surprise, we actually become the gift. We become the love that touches people — that changes people.

Next Christmas, if you want to hear "Hark the Herald Angels Sing" in four-and-a-half-part harmony, check out the Good Samaritan Nursing Home in Mountain Lake around six. Come join us — but only if you can carry a tune.

7

TONGUE TACOS

My wife and I pulled up in front of Greg Lemond's house. (Yep, the three-time winner of the Tour de France — that Lemond.) For a bike-aholic like me, this was hallowed ground. As we came up the driveway, it felt to me like the last loop on the Champs-Élysées with the Arc de Triomphe in the background. Mary told me to wipe the grin off my face before I got out of the car, because it was creeping her out.

Greg and his wife, Kathy, only live a few miles from us, but we had never been to their house.

I had met Kathy once before, in an interesting circumstance.

One afternoon in late November, a couple of friends and I went for a ride. As is our typical MO, we had miscalculated the duration of our trip. After fifty or sixty miles we were still about five miles from home when it went from dusk to dark, completely black. Not only that, but a thick fog had dropped in, and we could barely see each other.

A car pulled up alongside of us, slowed, then dropped back behind us and trailed us for about a half mile. It was spooky, like a B horror movie. When the car pulled alongside us again,

I almost expected to hear a chainsaw fire up. The window rolled down, and we heard this very non-Freddie-like woman say, "You guys can't do this, it's too dangerous. I'll pull over, you throw your bikes in my trunk, and I'll give you a ride home."

We told her we were just a few miles from home. We said, "We'll make it, don't worry." She couldn't get herself to leave us, so she drove her car behind us, lights flashing, the last few miles home. Talk about Be the Surprise.

Now, I would get to thank Kathy once again.

As for how we happened to be at the Lemond's house that day, we were sort of riding on the coattails of our daughter. Taylor knows their son, Scott, and we had been grandfathered in on her invitation to a graduation party for him. It seems the Lemond boys have always "appreciated" the Esau girls . . . from afar. Taylor was out of town that weekend, so we said we'd go for her . . . you know, I'm all about making sacrifices for my kids.

Greg and Kathy greeted us as if we were lifetime friends—that tells me that either Taylor is banking more social currency for us than we thought, or the Lemonds are just really nice people.

One of the first things Greg asked me was, "Did you get a taco yet?"

I hadn't, but I had seen the taco truck parked in the front yard, smoke puffing out of the pop-up chimney. It's hard to miss a taco truck in the heavily "uff da" populated 'burb of Orono. Evidently Greg had become a connoisseur of authentic Mexican tacos, and he had hired this real-life, south-of-the-border guy who travels around making this specialty from his taco RV. Greg and I walked up to the window, and he looked at me and said, "Have you ever tasted tongue tacos?"

"Say what?"

"Tongue. They're the best!"

I told him I hadn't, but as long as my taste buds were going to be sampling taste buds, let's get one for Mary and not tell her what it is. Greg thought that was an excellent idea.

We got our tacos and headed over to give Mary her surprise taste-of-a-taste treat. Greg was right; the tongue tacos were fabulous. Even Mary loved them. As she licked her fingers of the last juicy bit, Greg asked her what she thought it was she had just eaten.

"A taco, right? What?"

No clue.

"Tongue. You just ate your first tongue taco." Greg looked pleased, just like my older brother does after he plays a dirty trick on me. Mary started greening up like my lawn after the first ChemLawn treatment in spring.

I love surprises — the way they just reach out and grab you . . . sometimes by the tongue. I love it even more when I get to play a part in the surprising of someone else, when I get to help "grab the tongue."

Who knows what opportunities to Be the Surprise lay ahead. Kathy hadn't planned on running into three guys on a foggy night; it just happened. Greg didn't know Mary and I would be tongue taco virgins; we just wandered into his tasty trap. Maybe one of these days I'll be going about my business and a metaphorical fog will roll in, and I'll get a chance to Be the Surprise for Kathy and Greg too. I hope so.

On the way out, we saw a big basket of custom-made cycling socks. Turns out the Lemonds had had them designed with stitching to look just like their dog . . . a dog wearing a sweater and a little sombrero held on by a rubber band.

As we were walking out the door Scott handed four pairs to me and said, "Here, give these to Taylor."

If only a boy could win a girl's hand with socks.

8

THIS BIG

In September of 2006 a nasty tornado hit the small town of Rogers, Minnesota, leveling many homes and scattering debris everywhere. Afterward a pastor named Ben and about one hundred people from his congregation hit the neighborhood with chainsaws, shovels, and brooms and started doing whatever they could to help the victims.

Some helped look for lost items. Others went hunting for memories, things that held significance — pictures or jewelry. Several just stood with people, helping to find lost hope.

The governor of the state made an appearance that same day. When he found out that Ben was the pastor of this church of helpers, he went up to Ben and started making small talk. During the course of their discussion the governor asked Ben how big his church was. Ben scanned the area. Seeing all his people busy helping, he then looked back at the governor, spread his arms panoramically, and simply said, "Oh, about this big."

The size of this church was the size of its hearts.

The size of our hearts reflects the size of our God, and Be the Surprise is about the size of our love. Big God = Big Hearts = Magnanimous Fingers and Toes.

9

JOE'S CRAB SHACK GUY

It's Sunday. I got up early, walked our hound, Bailey, and prayed, *God, let me Be the Surprise today.*

I hopped into my plastic-sided Saturn and headed up to the church where I was speaking. I spend most of my Sunday mornings speaking in some church, somewhere, introducing the Surprise Me experiment to congregations. This morning it was a Free Church in Andover, Minnesota. I arrived early, so I had fifteen minutes to spare before the first service started. I walked into the back of the sanctuary and watched the crowd filtering in. The rows had clumps of people, families in some, others with individuals sitting alone.

As I scanned the room I thought, *I asked God to let me Be the Surprise today, I wonder if someone sitting here, right now, alone, needs someone to just say hi?*

I started walking down an aisle and noticed an older woman on my left. I almost made a turn toward her, but pulled up, thinking, *Yeah, she'll think I'm a bit weird walking up and stumbling out with, "Hi, I'm a Cancer. What's your sign?"*

So I kept on walking. Halfway to the front I saw a guy on my right, alone. For some reason, I sat down beside him. He had one of those shirts with a company name and logo embroidered on the front, so I said, "How's work going at, uh, Joe's Crab Shack?"

"I don't work there. It's just a shirt."

Not a great start. I knew I should have asked what his sign was. We talked a minute about nothing in particular. Then I glanced over at him and was surprised to see tears forming in his eyes.

"You doing okay?"

"Not really."

I asked if he wanted to talk about it, and he told me about his last year. Prison. Divorce. He'd lost custody of his twins, was jobless, hopeless. This was his first Sunday coming to church since prison and since, well, he couldn't remember when. I told him I wanted to help him, to be his friend. Tears gushed from his eyes. I could feel the weight of his sorrow and pain. It was years deep.

I had to leave because the service was starting, but I asked him to find me after the service. He did, and we talked for quite a while. I got his phone number, gave him a copy of my book, and said I'd call him on Monday. (I also gave his number to one of the elders and asked him to jump in to help this guy.)

I gave Joe's Crab Shack Guy a hug as we said good-bye, but he wouldn't let go. He was hanging on to me as if he would fall if I weren't holding on to him. His shoulders shook for a full minute. I got the impression that it was the first hug he had received in years.

It's weird how easy it is to find eager recipients of a listening ear or a simple hug. The world must be crammed with people just waiting for someone to care. I wonder how many — maybe every second or third person on the planet?

When I decided to do this experiment, I was trying to come up with the perfect question to ask people. You know, "If there was one thing I could do for you today, what would it be?"

But Being the Surprise might be so much simpler than that. It's probably more of a "Hi, how ya doing?" followed by a good chunk of listening.

§ § §

After the service I heard about some other things that were going on that morning. As I was talking to Joe's Crab Shack Guy, a guy was proposing to his girlfriend in the lobby of the church. I think they had met there or something, and this happened to be the Sunday he had chosen to propose. Kind of weird how it was the kick-off of the Surprise Me experiment, huh?

Then, the pastor told me that a guy had come up to him between services and said, "I just came here today to thank you."

"For what?" he asked.

"One year ago I was driving my motorcycle on this road in front of the church and was in a terrible accident. You were the first one on the scene, making sure I was taken care of. Well, I spent a lot of time in the hospital, but I'm doing much better, and I thought, 'Hey, I'll go check out that church where the pastor helped me.'"

So, that church's Surprise Me experiment got kicked off with an interesting trio of events. And all the while I was kicking off the Be the Surprise experiment, personally.

Surprise Me and Be the Surprise. It's going to be fun to see how these two sides of the same coin flip back and forth this month.

Receiving and giving. Giving and receiving.

Being and doing. Doing and being.

Loving God. Loving my neighbor.

SCULPTURES, STOGIES, AND STARGAZING

Paddle, HipWaders, and I were in Jackson Hole, Wyoming. We had just come from a nice dinner at a nice restaurant when we hatched this, uh, nice idea for a game. Every time we came across a sculpture of a bear, a moose, an eagle, or whatever, we would take turns striking poses that mirrored the sculpture. It was sort of a mime-meets-yoga-meets-Jim Carrey experience, and most of our still-life reenactments were of snarling grizzlies or friendly Bullwinkles.

My fellow competitors and I were taking this competition more seriously than was publicly acceptable, much to the dismay of our wives. We had asked them to serve as honorary judges, but it was hard to honor their judgments when they spent most of their time trying to flee the scene. (Just because other pedestrians, with no appreciation for art, weren't enjoying our "game" like we were, it didn't mean our competition wasn't a worthy endeavor. Many fellow side-walkers were willingly "spectating." I know because we got hearty smatterings of applause.)

The game fell apart after we found a five-bear sculpture and convinced our wives to join the grizzly mime fest. High art. Literally, it was similar to one of those pyramids that cheerleaders build. (I have a picture of this, proof positive, as well as a picture of the actual sculpture. You can hardly tell our cluster apart from the bronze version — other than the two-inch incisors.)

Sure, Paddle and H-Waders are a bit crazy (my wife claims they're a bad influence on me . . . their wives claim the reverse), but the three of us have some wonderfully deep conversations. We had one that night under the starlight.

Upon our return to the cabin, we decided to go for a walk. Paddle passed out the stogies and we walked out the door into a world of blackness. We stepped cautiously down the driveway, stogies serving as flashlights, until our eyes grew more accustomed to the darkness. We got out to the road, away from the overhanging trees, and looked up to see God showing off with his myriad galaxies, planets, and stars.

As we walked and talked, we couldn't tear our eyes away from the heavens. I had never seen the Big Dipper so deep, the Milky Way so milky, and Orion so, so . . . I don't even know what or where Orion is, I just wanted to sound smart.

As I was saying, we walked and talked and after about fifteen minutes, our necks were sore. It's hard to walk with your head cranked back that far. Finally, I just laid down in the middle of the road. Waders looked at me and said, "What are you doing?"

"Making it easier to look at the stars."

Pause.

"You're just going to lie down in the middle of the road?" Waders asked.

"Yup."

About that time Paddle laid down.

It took a few moments, but Waders finally caved because I convinced him that we'd hear and see a car coming from a long ways off on a night this black and silent — at *least* a good five seconds before it hit us.

The three of us spent about a half hour sprawled between the white lines of the highway. No cars came. We saw a couple of shooting stars. I made a wish, but didn't say anything. I don't know if they wished or not.

As I lay there, puffing my cigar just often enough to keep it lit, I thought about the road I've traveled so far in my life. I'm not a frequent recliner. I barrel down my roadway, dragging along my agendas and ambitions, rarely stopping for a good, long look. Oh, I glance up. I regularly peek at God. But do I often crank my head back and just stare? Not really.

I'm a God-glancer. I don't often gaze long enough to know the whereabouts of his constellations, his roadmap for my life. I know the Dipper and the North Star, but he's got a lot more detail he'd like to fill in.

I think it's going to be hard to Be the Surprise if I'm only casually glancing at the one who cues those surprises. If I want to be God's sculpture, his reenactment here on earth, I'll need to spend time staring at him, studying the original that I'm trying to emulate.

If I want to look like the real thing, I need to become a recliner. I need to pull up, lie down between the white lines, and study the face of the only one who can make me become enough like him so that I can authentically be his art in this world.

I stood and brushed the road pebbles from my jeans as we made our way back to the cabin. Sure, we had fun imitating sculptures of grizzlies tonight, but I want my whole life to be carved into a loving likeness of the only one worthy of imitation.

All that thinking distracted me — my stogie just went out.

11

LOVE SEAT

When Mary and I walked into the Jackson Hole airport we happened upon a PG-13 love scene. A liberal interpretation of PG-13, that is. This young couple was making out as if ChapStick came in foot-long dispensers. One of them was obviously leaving and one staying.

We gawked for a moment, then moved on.

We were heading home from our long weekend in Wyoming with the Paddles and the HipWaders. While they had tickets and boarding passes, we had, well, class-5 standby status — the airline equivalent of slim-to-none (and slim seemed lost in the labyrinth of unclaimed baggage).

Mary works part-time for Northwest Airlines, so we occasionally have the pleasure of pretending to be flying somewhere — maybe, at a given time, sorta. We looked at the ticket agent with that "What-are-our-chances?" look. She smirked and gave us the forecast for the next day in the Hole. The flight was seriously overbooked.

We said good-bye to our friends and sat down to wait.

The last person to board was Loverboy from the aforementioned PG-13 scene. He didn't have any cheek tears, but his eyes were all glossied up and red. Parting is such sweet sorrow; keep the daggers and poison away from these two.

The last passenger had boarded; the gate was now empty.

We were hovering around the ticket agent, hoping she would call our names. A number of people hadn't shown up, but she still gave us little hope.

Then it happened. She called our name. Kinda.

"Ee-sooo-aah?" Was she calling hogs — or us?

"Ee-saw?" I said, trying to confirm that we were the people formerly known as the Eesoooaahs.

"I've got one ticket, one seat left," she said, "Do one of you want it?"

This is the decision we hate. Divide and conquer, or not. Who stays, who goes? Rock, paper, scissors?

Mary and I took two giant steps forward, and said we were going to both stay and try to get on a flight the next morning.

"Tomorrow doesn't look much better," stated the ticket agent, well-trained in the art of gloom. The door closed on the Jetway, and we turned to walk away. We had no place to stay, no car, no plans. The key to Paddle's cabin was on the plane.

It was about then that the Jetway door burst open.

Loverboy!

Evidently it's true — absence, however abbreviated, *does* make the heart grow fonder. He walked confidently up to the ticket agent and slapped his boarding pass on the counter.

"I'm *not* going," he said, jaw set. She told him that he probably couldn't get a refund. He didn't give a rat's patutti. His girlfriend, still watching through the glass window of the gate, looked a bit like one of those birds that keeps flying into the picture window, frustrated by the transparent force field.

I don't think L-Boy, this master of smooch, even knew we existed, let alone that we wanted his seat. As he turned to join Juliet, I grabbed his arm, slapped a twenty spot in his palm, and said, "Take her out to dinner." One surprise deserves another.

The guy had just thrown away three hundred bucks, so I don't think he cared all that much about my twenty, but he kept it, thanked me, spun on his heel, and headed toward happiness. Roll credits.

The ticket agent looked at us with a look that said, "Geez Louise — you might want to consider buying some lottery tickets today." We boarded the plane to the cheers of the Paddles and HipWaders. Some days the sun just seems to shine on our sculptures. Some days it trickles back to us.

As I settled into seat 8B, the seat that love gave, I turned and planted a PG-13er on my wife.

Ain't love grand?

12

MOWING FOR AFFIRMATION

I mow for affirmation. Sure, a manicured lawn looks better, but I'm not a trimmer-wielding, fescue pedicurist at heart. Long or short, it's all the same to me.

I mow because I like the "Thanks, Ter. Good job" I get afterward. Every week when my bluegrass buddies stretch beyond the dreaded four-inch mark, I fire up my Yardman riding mower and give the boys a haircut. Then, when my wife pulls up our driveway to a freshly coiffed lawn, she smiles, gives me a treat, pats me on the head, and I feel good. I do a lot of things for affirmation, not so much because I'm a good guy, but because I like the strokes that come with being a good-thing-doer.

I'm aware of the danger of performing for treats. My dog is a slave to Milk-Bone. She'll do almost anything for a doggie treat. If I become treat-driven, I will have, in effect, become the performing pet of whoever offers the juiciest, tastiest treats. Since I don't really want to become *that* much like my dog, I decided to see if I could mow the lawn just to honor my wife, beautify the neighborhood, make the world a better place . . . *sans* treat.

So, tonight while Mary was gone at a meeting, I fired up my Yardman riding mower and gave the boys a butch. By the time I was halfway through, it was dark — really dark. The finishing loops were guesswork. When my wife got home, the lawn was cut — after a fashion. Of course, she couldn't see the random Mohawk-ish outcroppings where I had missed six inches here and there; it was dark, so dark she couldn't even tell the lawn had been mowed.

She didn't even notice.

I mean, shouldn't she have smelled it? After all, freshly cut grass has a rather distinct odor.

Okay, okay. I guess the goal of Be the Surprise is not the recognition of the surprise-or, but the gifting to the surprise-ee. One thing I hope to make progress on with this spiritual experiment is to stop looking to be congratulated for my exemplary philanthropy.

I know what you are thinking: *Exemplary? You mowed the lawn, Esau! It's not like you negotiated peace in Darfur. Humility?*

Speaking of humility, this morning I read a chapter in a book called *The Mountain of Silence*. It's the story of a Greek monk who was becoming quite a big deal, the talk of the monastery and community. Here's what he had to say about his rise in popularity. "My greatest enemy is my reputation. Woe to the monk who gets famous."[2]

Yeah, but did he mow the entire lawn — in the *dark*?

49

13

DREAMING

I've been working with this life coach for the last three months. I never thought I'd be one of those guys who says, ". . . and then my life coach said to me . . ." Never thought it would happen. But it did.

This life coach, who I didn't know was a life coach, called me one day and set up a lunch because he had just had a book published and wanted to pick my brain on how to help market it. By the end of the lunch I informed him that he didn't need me as much as I needed him. So I hired him . . . on the spot, for a three-month stint.

He's been helping me in a lot of ways, but the thing that impacted me the most was what he asked me in our very first session: "Tell me about your dreams for the rest of your life."

I began with some modest stuff and started getting more and more grandiose, but I kept pulling back, saying, "Well, I know this sounds ridiculous, but . . ." Every time I said that, he would stop me and say, "Dreams don't come in boxes. Dreams shouldn't be practical. Dreams should maybe even appear unattainable. Never, never put limits on your dreams." Tim encouraged me to think bigger than I ever have.

Talk about a freeing experience. All my life I've felt compelled to dream manageable dreams, to come down to reality and stop being so idealistic — unrealistic. Tim refused to listen to truncated, bite-sized, digestible dreams.

I went on for an hour. Spouting the most outrageous, improbable, fantastic vision of what *could be* if I won the lottery and was able to harness every ounce of my brain, and if I could clone myself — ten times — and, well, you get the idea.

Lest you think I'm nuts to live my life in the netherworld of "what if" and "make believe," let me say that I do realize that dreams have to be bitten off in manageable chunks. It takes a well-planned strategy and sound tactics to frame up the walls of our dreams. We can't just live in our hopes and expect to never wake up. If we do, we will wake up to unfulfilled dreams. However, until we dream fully and freely, we won't even *want* to wake up. We won't have anything to wake up to. Too many of us live lives that are patched together with limits, qualifiers, rules, and "good enoughs."

I've got two words for you. *Re — sist!*

§ § §

I had dinner with some friends a while back. We were talking about dreams. One friend said that he and his wife had sat down and decided what lifestyle they wanted to live and *then* did some dream planning around that. I know this sounds harsh and idealistic, but I don't think these people are surprise ready. They aren't ready to be nudged out of the nest and to fly on their God-given dreams. It's more like they have chosen a nearby branch to safely land on.

If God intended flight, and he did, we can't settle for short bursts of flapping and never actually soar. I think part of Being the Surprise is helping free people to dream all that is in them, all that God is stirring inside. If we can encourage people to dream with a greater sense of freedom, without fear — which is what God wants ("perfect love casts out fear" (1 John 4:18, NASB) — then that would be one of the cooler gifts we could start passing out.

The freedom to dream is a nebulous thing, hard to quantify, but it's definitely a gift of great value, a tangible intangible, if you know what I mean. I'm going to look for more ways to Be the Surprise in intangible ways.

§ § §

I had lunch with Booker today. He showed up, we ordered some pasta, and grabbed a table outside. I asked him how his love life was. He said good. I said really? He said yeah.

Then I asked him about his job. He said it was good, but this time the good was less convincing.

I wondered if he was struggling with giving himself permission to dream, so I asked him, "What would you like to be doing with your life? What do you want your life to be about ... from now to the end? What *are* your dreams?" After two months of working with a life coach I'm starting to act like one. This could be dangerous. People should probably not listen to me.

But Booker did. I'm twenty years older than he is, so he probably thinks I know some stuff. He said he wanted time to think about this dream question. "Next lunch I'll tell you," he said. And he will.

I don't know the specifics of Booker's dream, but I think I've got a good idea of the character of it. I've known him long enough to know what revs his soul. I know he wants to be involved in people's lives. He wants to give and help and care . . . to Be the Surprise in people's lives. Sooner or later he'll need a street where he can open up the throttle and let it run. If he doesn't, he's going to muck up his carburetor.

Life is meant to run on the clean fuel of our soul's desires and purpose, our God-installed desires and purposes. If we settle for cheap fuel so we can buy a bigger lifestyle, we may look like we're riding in style, but it never *feels* that way. It's like that '87 Jaguar I used to own — it may have looked cool, but it was little more than a dressed-up hunk of non-functionality.

I think Booker wants the souped-up engine in a less ostentatious body. He knows what he wants. What's more, he wants what God wants. I've got a lot of faith in Booker because his soul is drawn to the pure stuff. He's about to give himself permission to become surprise ready.

§ § §

Okay, here's the *qualifier* on this whole dream thing. Are you ready?

Dreams can very easily become ambitions. Ambitions can become agendas. Agendas, wants. Wants, cravings. And the sauce reduction continues till all that's left in the pan is *us* — *our* wants, *our* agendas, *our* ambitions. When this happens, we have ceased to dream. We have deluded ourselves into thinking we can plan our own future. We are pursuing our own dreams so they will become reality.

But what if our realities have been flip-flopped?

Try this on — if we pursue *God*, his dreams become our dreams, and will ultimately pursue *us*. When we draw near to God, he draws his/our dreams near to us. Dream recognition happens only when we are looking through the windshield of the vehicle that God is driving. Dreams are the things we pursue *with* God — him driving, us shotgun. They are what lie in our paths when we are going the same direction as God — him steering. He can and will deliver us to our dreams if we stay seated, stay with/beside him. Only then can he direct the surprises and the person attempting to Be the Surprise. God drives both Surprise Me and Be the Surprise. Remove him from the process and we're in an agenda-driven pursuit.

Pursuing dreams without looking through the God-filter is like staring at the sun. If we want to see what's ahead of us, we need to let the sun illumine it, let the sun do its job. God's job is to direct us. We need to let him do his job.

As he illumines our path, we walk.

As he reveals our dreams, we pursue.

So dream all you want, but don't dream alone. Dream with. Dream beside. Dream shotgun.

Be the Surprise . . . from the passenger seat.

14

LESS TAKE, MORE GIVE

We've all heard religious people say, "Let's take America back for God!" There's talk of mobilizing, arming, fighting, and overcoming. And the cheers go up.

Does it seem to you that faith talk is sounding more and more militaristic? That kind of talk makes me nervous.

Oh, I'm all for mobilizing — hearts, not causes.

I'm all for taking up arms — to hold, not harm.

I'm all for fighting — fighting the perception that some people don't deserve our love, not fighting those very people.

Overcoming? Why not, as long as it means overcoming my need to feel good about myself by elevating me over you.

Be the Surprise is bigger than taking America back for God.

It's *giving* ourselves *back to God*.

It's saying, "Rather than confront, challenge, and protest *against* people, I'm going to love and care *for* those very same people, regardless of our differing views on issues. If I'm going to get militaristic about something, it's going to be to 'act justly, to love mercy, and walk humbly with my God' (Micah 6:8, paraphrased)."

What if we surprise the world, not by strong-arming people into moralistic conformity, but by loving them without regard to their morality, conformity, or any other "-ity" we can think of? Human beings are not our enemies — never have been. But even if they were our enemies, aren't they the ones Jesus asked us to love — especially them?

Wouldn't the world be shocked if Christians all started giving back? If we stopped competing. Stopped brown-nosing. Stopped judging. Wouldn't that just totally mess with the heads of this culture?

If we all really *gave* ourselves back to God, I'm not sure how much *taking back* of America would be necessary.

I'm not the only one who thinks that way. I saw a wall plaque the other day that said, "Live in such a way that those who know you but don't know God, will come to know God — because they know you."

Less take, more give.

15

YARDIE

I started this experiment thinking it would go along smoothly and that I would finish it in thirty days, just like I had when I did the Surprise Me experiment. I was wrong. I quit about halfway through. Here's what happened.

Two things.

First, I realized that Being the Surprise was a whole lot harder and more time consuming than I had expected. *Being the Surprise* is so much more work than simply *observing* the surprises. The Surprise Me experiment was about awareness, seeing, recognizing. This experiment is about, well—being, engaging, committing.

Harder, much harder.

And, I realized something else. Two weeks into this experiment I realized I had ignored my family because I was so busy being the loving, helping, benevolent fingers and toes of Jesus to everyone I met . . . well, that is, everyone except for my family.

I started stressing out because I felt the family divide growing—distance and disconnection. "But I'm on a mission," I told myself. "I'm fighting for a greater cause — the Experiment, the Book. Don't they understand that? Can't they let me run for one month? Can't they tolerate stranger status for a measly thirty days? Come on!"

Turns out, I couldn't tolerate myself for treating my family that way.

If I can't Be the Surprise for the people I love the most, if I can't first Be the Surprise for the people I live with, for my wife and daughters, then I'm faking it with the others. It's wrong. It's religious duty that's gotten screwed up. It's everything that I have always hated.

So I quit.

I felt terribly guilty about it, but my guilt over the phoniness of what the experiment was becoming, over who I was becoming, was greater than my pre-programmed mode to never quit what I start.

I just had a weird thought. *What if God sort of planned this failure?* Think about it. What if he interrupts even our invitation to him to interrupt us? Whoa. Convoluted. If I'm going to be true to the concept of living in a heightened state of spiritual awareness, then I need to honor the collapse of what I *think* I'm doing for God—this experiment.

Maybe I also need to lose the stigma of failure. After all, it's a common, universal condition. We fail. We *all* fail. Maybe if we saw failure, even in authors—excuse me, in *Christian* authors—a bit more, it might be a healthy thing. Just because I happen to be writing books doesn't mean I get what all this is about any better than you do. We're all muddling along, seeing dimly. Maybe one of the necessary ingredients of reality spirituality is failure.

I don't want to be spiritually arrogant. I want to be viewed as a guy who has a heart for God, who desires him with all that is in me. But that doesn't keep me from banging into curbs and stubbing my toes and stepping on my tongue and frequently losing my way when the batteries on my spiritual GPS run low. Still, God speaks to me, through me, with me. Still, he loves me and holds me. Still, he preps the fatted calf.

I fail, but he doesn't dispose of me.

§ § §

My fourteen-year-old Yardman riding mower has health issues. He's failing. I'd like to get a new mower with some horse that still has power, then I'd put my faithful old Yardman out to pasture.

But he beat me to it; a month ago my Yardman put himself out to pasture. Eighteen-and-a-half horses in a deep, deep coma. They shoot horses, don't they? I wish there was a cliff close by; I'd like to *Thelma and Louise* this thing! To dispose of him.

I put him on life support for a couple of hours, plugged him into a battery charger, but his eyes are still rolled back. The headlights are on, but nobody's home.

I'm not sure what to do with Yardie. A repairman said it would probably take eight rolls of green to fix him, and I'm not talking sod rolls here. Yardie won't fit in my garbage can. I don't think I can donate a dead mower to Goodwill. He's too big and smelly to be a coffee table. Mary half-seriously suggested I take my ax, chop the Y-Man into manageable pieces, and smuggle him into the trash week-by-week. Seems a bit cold-hearted. After years of the Y-Man hauling the T-Boy around my two acres, I ax-murder him? Not much gratitude there.

Yesterday I made a new purchase — the cheapest Honda push mower I could buy at Costco. It's amazing how efficient this little Honda is. It takes longer, but it cuts better, closer, and cleaner. It uses less gas. Makes less noise. It has never gouged the lawn — ever. I couldn't say that about Yardie — never.

Still, I miss Yardie.

I looked over the top of his yellow hood for fourteen years. I wonder how many circles we completed together during that time? I knew the patterns we made in the grass. I knew how far to shift my weight to the right on the steep ditch. I knew that he could turn much sharper to the left than the right, so I planned my turns to work with him. I knew his quirks and some days it seemed he knew mine.

We worked well together.

§ § §

Slowly, surely, I'm learning to work well with God. Oh, he knows my failings. He has seen me take gouges out of people. He knows I turn left better than right.

But he still uses me. I'm starting to think God is *partial* to failures — not just tolerant, but *partial*. When I fail he picks me up, dusts me off, and gives me even *greater* trust and responsibility. Amazing. I'm a klutz God relishes to use. I'm a bumbler he honors with tasks that stupefy me. He puts me in places where I get to touch for him, see for him, and perhaps even speak for him.

Yeah, I'm going to fail at completing the Be the Surprise experiment in thirty days, but what if I'm not supposed to knock this thing out with a sound-byte, drive-through efficiency? What if *being* is more invasive than that? What if *being* takes more time, *needs* more time?

I think I have subconsciously been substituting doing for being. *Do* the surprise. Perform. Hop to. Prove. Earn. Enough. Validate.

Maybe I jumped to "do" because it's easier than "be." I can track "do." I can measure what I've *done*, but gauging what I am *becoming* is a bit trickier. Was I substituting activity for authenticity? When "do" takes the place of "be," we invariably set ourselves up for failure.

I'm going to fire up this experiment again. I'm getting back on the horse. I want to get back to Being the Surprise, even if it's in my own, unique, flawed sort of way. The beauty of this is that our flawed-ness does not disqualify us for God's purposes; rather, our humanity perfectly matches us to his sufficiency and love.

I'm going to try again. I'm not sure if I'll start over or take up where I left off. But I'm not going to ignore my family this time. I think I need to "be" for them first. If I can't, I'll quit again.

16

THE SLIDE SHOW

One of my first post "I quit" actions was to book my dad for a slide show. I'd thought about doing this for years but had always seemed too busy to make it happen. Dad and I lived the Cat Steven's "Cats in the Cradle" scenario more closely than I like to admit. Enough of that pattern. If I feel nudged to do something, I need to let that nudge move me.

So I sent the invitation:

> Hey guys,
>
> I'm planning a party, guys only. I'm inviting my dad to spend an evening showing his slides of his experiences in WW II. He's got unbelievable pictures and stories — liberating concentration camps, Battle of the Bulge, bullet holes in the windshield of the wrecker he drove, plus a million others. He loves to tell stories and he's pretty dang good at it for an eighty-seven-year-old. This is a chance for me to honor my dad in a way that he really deserves, and in a way he will understand. I'm not sure how many years

he has left, so I'm excited to finally be doing this. I should have done it years ago.

We're doing it at our house on Thursday, June 22nd, 7 p.m.

Hope you can all make it. I'm sure we'll have drinks and some snacks, but *I'm* doing this, not Mary, so don't expect any *foie gras* or truffles.

Thanks guys,
Terry

And so my buddies came. Packed out our family room.

My dad fired up the old slide projector and it was Show and Tell with a military twist.

Dad came from a town filled with German Mennonite immigrants. Most of them went into the service with a CO status, meaning they were conscientious objectors opting not to serve in combat because of a religious belief opposed to violence. My dad didn't carry that belief and hadn't signed up that way, but because he had entered with the group from Mountain Lake, CO had been stamped on his file.

His commander thought it was a mistake, so he told one of his other officers, "I'm going to invite Esau into my office, then I'm going to throw my pistol at him. If he catches it, he goes with us to Europe, if not, he stays home." Dad caught the pistol. (Now you know the tricky selection process our military goes through when selecting soldiers.)

Dad told us about welding a rod to the front end of his truck. It stuck straight up about four feet. He said he did that because the Germans sometimes would string piano wire between trees, about neck-high, so when trucks would come cruising by the wire would decapitate a soldier who wasn't watching.

We saw pictures of the Battle of the Bulge — tracers going through the night sky, tanks blown apart, knee-deep mud, anti-aircraft guns firing, planes falling. Ominous images frozen in time, sepia scenes from a black-and-white war — real moments from an unreal world that none of us had ever been forced to experience.

His battalion was the first to come upon the concentration camps, and he showed us pictures of what they found, raw pictures of bodies stacked like cordwood. Ditches filled with men, women, and children — some killed minutes before the U.S. Army arrived. And he showed us a picture of the commander of this camp, lying dead beside his bicycle. The commander, after realizing his day was over, changed into civilian clothes and hopped on a bike and tried to pretend he was one of the locals. It didn't work.

Dad told of the Germans parachuting in, behind their lines, wearing U.S. Army military-issue uniforms. He told of the confusion this caused.

He talked a little about fear and exhaustion. He talked a lot about mission and purpose. He talked about a faith that sustained him and a God who walked with him through minefields and trenches and foxholes.

He showed pictures of downtown Paris on the day the war ended. It was a huge party — dancing, hugging, kissing. I think my dad might have found a random French girl or two to kiss. That may have been the friendliest day in the history of

Franco-American relations.

I saw my dad differently that night. I saw him through the eyes of all of my buddies. Eyes that looked on with awe and respect. To me he was always Dad, you know, the guy I had to ask to use the car before a date. The guy who made the rules and made sure I kept them. Tonight he wasn't that guy. He grew in my eyes tonight.

When God scratched his top-ten list in the stone tablets back on Mt. Sinai, one of his biggies was "Honor your father and mother." Why is that one so easy to overlook? This night was one of the few times in my life where I actually pulled that off. I think Dad walked away feeling honored. Fifteen men from twenty to fifty-five hung on his every word. They asked him questions. They applauded. After two hours they thanked him, not just for showing his slides, but also for serving in the Army and protecting their freedom. Sincere gratitude and respect.

Dad's chin rode a bit higher, his chest a bit fuller. He heard that he mattered, that he was appreciated. At eighty-seven he discovered he can still touch lives. He needed that. We all need it.

(Two months later.)

I just found out last night that my dad has a valve in his heart that is functioning poorly. They'd like to do surgery but feel he's not strong enough to survive it. So they told him to live out the days he has left, to enjoy them and take what he gets.

I asked him last night how he felt about that prognosis. "Pretty good," he said. "I've had eighty-seven good years, far more than most." I asked him if he had some things he wanted to do with the time he has left. He said, "Well, for starters, I want to drive up there and have lunch with you."

I think we may have let the cat out of the cradle.

17

PHILO*SELF*IZING

I just finished reading an interesting novel called *The Fountainhead*. It's old — a classic written by Ayn Rand, published in 1943. On the dustcover it says, "This book is based on a challenging belief in the importance of selfishness, on the provocative idea that man's ego is the fountainhead of human progress." It seems terribly fitting that immediately after I finished reading this book I would undertake a spiritual experiment that is a full pendulum swing in the opposite direction. This experiment is rooted in the belief of the importance of self-*less*-ness.

Just to clarify, let me say I don't believe in the "oh, woe is me, I am nothing, please, step all over me because I am of little or no consequence in the world" mentality. I know some people of faith who hold that view, but they aren't reading the same Bible as I am.

If God wanted a world full of self-less, personality-less, will-less mannequins, he could have created them with both hands tied behind his back. But he didn't. He believes in Self. He custom-built the Self into each of us. When it comes to Self, there are no dups, copies, lithographs, or replications. We are his signed works of Self art.

Not only did God give each of us an original Self, but he also put a dash of his own Self into us. So, yes, we are paintings that hang on his wall — he's got one of those nifty little lights above each painting to show off the colors and texture. He's proud of the masterpieces in his gallery — us.

So being selfless has little to do with the reduction or diminution of Self. That's a slap in the face of the artist who created us. Belittle the art, belittle the artist.

I think the proper view of Self is to see ourselves as God sees us — of infinite worth and value. When we begin to see ourselves in that way — his way — we become conspicuously free from the need to self-criticize or the need to self-promote, because if God already highly values us, and we accept his appraisal, then we will no longer need to solicit affirmation from everyone we meet. We already have it, from God. We already *feel* valuable.

A healthy God-view of Self frees us to live with less emphasis *on* Self. It enables us to look beyond our *Selves*, to be unconcerned about whether our personal star is rising or falling. If I am secure in my own Self-value, I can spend my energy building the Self-esteem of others — knowing that in building them up, it does not diminish me. Rather, the more I elevate others, the better I feel about my Self.

18

TEN BUCKS FOR PARKING

Not long ago I was scheduled to speak at the Christian Community Fair, which was being held in the St. Paul Civic Center. The huge space could easily have handled twenty thousand browsers, but there looked to be only about a thousand people — a tad short of the expected turnout.

The Minneapolis/St. Paul Christian community had come together to hear speakers, authors, and Christian recording artists. And, of course, they had come to view the standard row upon row of booths selling a quirky conglomeration of got-to-have-it, can't-live-without-it Jesus junk: bumper stickers warning people of driverless cars in case of the Rapture, suncatchers with clever sayings, Christian self-help books (isn't that an oxymoron?), bobble-headed Jesus dolls, and even poker chips with Bible verses. "I'll see your Romans 8:28 and raise you a John 3:16."

I walked into my assigned room where I was supposed to speak in about five minutes and saw that most of the 250 seats were empty. Two people were sitting in my section; one was already dozing off, the other listing in that direction. Neither looked as if they had arrived with any degree of intentionality, eagerly anticipating my nuggets of wisdom.

The guy running the sound asked what I would like for a mic. At first I thought he was joking. The speaker before me was a comedian and was working his crowd of four, blasting jokes like bullets from an Uzi. Oh, he was killing them all right. Laughs need critical mass, and his four-person mass was, uh, critically unamused. I empathized with him because I know what it feels like to bomb.

Five minutes after I was supposed to be on, I saw that my "crowd" had grown to six. "Woo hoo! Ushers, set up the closed-circuit camera for the overflow in the lobby. Quickly!"

I thought about sneaking off and pretending that I had never been there. But I knew that would be a cop-out, so I corralled all six people in the audience, put some chairs in a circle, and said, "So, let's introduce ourselves."

It was a small group, one of the best ones I've ever been a part of.

One person in particular seemed to be the reason that we were there. Kristine. She told us how she had just moved to Minneapolis with her two kids a couple of weeks before. She was recently divorced and had left her job as a dancer in Houston and come to Minnesota to start over, in life and faith. Her ex-in-laws had offered to take her kids for the night, a rare occasion, and had handed her a ten-dollar bill as she left, an even more rare happening. The ten was all the money Kristine had to her name. Maybe she would get a cheap dinner, maybe a little gas for her car — the options were endless.

She told us she got in her car and started driving to nowhere in particular. As she passed downtown St. Paul, she thought she had better turn around because her gas was getting low. As she made the loop, she turned on her radio to a station that was new to her . . . the local Christian radio station. An ad for the Christian Community Fair came on and Kristine heard the magic word — *free.* The announcer then said, "It's in downtown St. Paul at the Civic Center." She looked up and saw that the Civic Center was straight ahead.

When she drove into the parking lot, she saw a sign that read, "Event parking — $10." Ouch. She handed the attendant everything she had, walked in, and prayed, *God, you must have something for me here, so . . .*

She ended up in my section because, well, there were chairs available.

She talked about all the struggles she'd been through in the last few years and how God seemed to be wedging himself into her life. And she was welcoming him, wanting him to come, but needing help connecting. This group was perfectly suited to help her with that. One couple encouraged Kristine in ways that amazed me, as if they had been prepped for this young woman. Another man lived near Kristine and knew the church where she had been attending. He told her that he would help her connect with people there.

Almost two hours later we broke up; I had been scheduled to speak for forty-five minutes. As I was packing up my stuff, the speaker following me, seeing the empty room, came up to me and said, "What's going on? Where is everybody?"

I said, "This is it. The guy before me had four, I had six . . . you're a much bigger name, you should have at least eight."

He reached for his cell phone. "This is ridiculous! I'm not speaking to chairs." He started looking for the number for the director of the community fair to give him a piece of his mind. He paced, he fumed. He didn't stick around that night. I knew how he felt. I had been moments from making the exact same decision.

Luckily, and surprisingly, I stayed.

Sometimes the potential for us to Be the Surprise looks pathetic. Sometimes it looks suspiciously as if God doesn't have a clue what he's doing. And don't let me fool you . . . there are many times, including the one I just told you about, when I could swear that God had miscalculated, badly — with me.

But be warned.

Don't judge too hastily. God doesn't schedule poorly. His marketing may be a bit unorthodox (i.e. ex-in-laws, a ten-spot in hand, a precisely-timed radio ad, the aligning of an event with the location of a car, the ten-dollar parking, the free fair . . . even a small turnout that allowed for a personal, small-group setting) but God's methods are spot-on — if we don't abort his appointment because we are three people short of a quorum.

God is up to something. Always is, always has been, and he has always invited us into that something. Being the Surprise sometimes requires us to ride a meaningless situation long enough to find out if it is as pointless as it appears.

Want more proof? A month after this experience I got the following e-mail from Kristine:

> Good Friday morning, Terry!!
> I'm not sure whether you'll remember me

or not, but you and your words certainly left an impression on me. :)

I met you at the Christian Community Fair about a month ago. You and I, as well as four other people, brought our chairs together and shared in a couple of hours of stories and discussion . . . it was truly a blessing. What I didn't tell all of you was that I was going to be baptized the following Sunday evening. Your stories and the insight spoken of by you, as well as the other people that were there, were an inspiration to this new Christian, preparing for her first act of obedience in being baptized.

I will begin my own 30-day journal, starting tomorrow . . . I had gone about two weeks praying the prayer just after meeting you, but never journaled . . . wish I would have, because they were incredible.

My journey as a Christian thus far has been full of tremendous struggles . . . all through which I've learned to lift up my eyes, filled with tears or not, and praise the God that saved me. Sometimes, it's still so overwhelming, but I'm truly looking forward to starting my own Surprise Me journal tomorrow. I don't take that simple prayer lightly. Our God is so incredibly powerful and profound, and opening ourselves up to be his constant vessel is

73

an intense undertaking, and a journey that I know will be profound, indeed.

I haven't stopped thinking about you since that night, and simply wanted to steal this opportunity to say thank you . . . you and your stories were a gift, and a "surprise" of my own.

Kristine

Like I said, sometimes Being the Surprise requires us to bury our pride, circle some chairs, and sift through the dull till the brilliance is revealed.

19

REALLY FRIENDLY MONKS

Monks in certain orders, when they meet each other along the path, bow and honor each other, often by kissing each other's hand. Seems odd. Today I read the reason they do this. They believe that whenever you meet someone, in reality, you meet God. As such, you honor that person because you have in front of you the very presence of God. Wouldn't it turn the world all catawampus if we all started doing this? Not the kissing thing, that's a bit much, but just honoring each other's presence as if it were God's. Try it on for a day. I think I will.

20

TENSION

Two months after my book *Surprise Me* came out, I got an invitation to speak at Baylor University in Waco, Texas. They had had a last-minute cancellation and the campus pastor, Byron, e-mailed and asked me to fill in. He knew a bit about my book and thought it might be a good message for the Baylor students.

I accepted the invitation and told Byron that we had been planning on visiting Baylor that very weekend in order to see our middle daughter, Lauren, who is a student there. Not only would I get paid to visit my daughter, I would also be able to share my passion with thousands of Baylor students.

The day before we left for Texas, I got an e-mail from a local pastor in Waco, Kyle Lake, saying that his church was going to be starting the Surprise Me experiment on Sunday. I replied, saying that, oddly enough, I was going to be in Waco that Sunday. He asked me to attend his church and said he'd like to introduce me and ask a few questions during the service.

Mary and I arrived in Waco. On Saturday morning I ran into Kyle at Baylor's homecoming parade. He walked up to me, grabbed my hand, and shook it vigorously, saying how excited he was to be starting this experiment and to have me there. I had only met Kyle once, about nine months earlier, for maybe a total of sixty seconds, so I was impressed that he had identified me in a crowd of thousands at the parade.

The next morning we showed up at his church. The first part of the service was devoted to introducing the experiment. Ben, the associate pastor, explained the concept as the book was displayed on the overhead screens. He issued the challenge for the entire church to pray, *Surprise me, God*, every morning for the next thirty days.

Ten minutes later, after the band had played a few tunes, Kyle stepped into the baptistery to perform a baptism. When he was chest-deep in the water, he reached to adjust the mic. Evidently, as was discovered later, the baptistery had some significant electrical wiring problems, and when Kyle touched the mic, he got a shock, dropped the mic into the water, and then . . .

Kyle was electrocuted, right there, in front of his congregation. One thousand college students watched in horror.

I sat in my chair, dumbfounded. As the chaos swirled around us — the attempts to revive Kyle, the ambulance showing up — I looked on in total disbelief. Was this really happening? All I could think was, *Please, let this be a dream.*

It wasn't.

I've never seen God as an ornery ol' cuss with an axe to grind. I've never viewed him as vindictive, vengeful, or sadistic. I've never felt as if he were out to get me — us. But that morning I had to wrestle with those views like never before.

How does God expect us to be his

hands and feet when we see people like Kyle living that out in amazing ways and yet getting cut down in their prime? How do we keep these kinds of surprises from derailing us?

My initial reaction was anger, intense anger that I somehow managed to keep bottled up. I wanted to break something, but it's hard to break things inconspicuously when you're in church. Then my anger morphed into confusion and intense sadness. Guilt. Then grief.

I asked God a lot of the big, hard questions that morning — in a more forceful way than I've asked them in the past. But the concrete answers eluded me. They still do. I still don't understand.

Needless to say, one of the more difficult things I've had to do in my life was speaking in chapel at Baylor the next day. I suggested to Byron, the campus pastor, that he replace me with someone who knew Kyle better or who could help the students deal with their grief. But Byron said there were too many *coincidences* that had brought me to Waco that weekend. He believed God wanted to say something to the students through me.

I didn't want to be that guy. I didn't want to walk on stage in front of those students, but I knew Byron was right. The timing of my visit was not *coincidental*.

I can't remember what I said that morning, but I tried to be honest and vulnerable about where I was and what I thought and believed at that moment. I hope it helped the students wrestle with their loss. I hope it gave them permission to ask the questions that they were undoubtedly thinking. I don't think God was, or ever will be, intimidated by our questions. From what I've read about Kyle, that's what he believed too.

But, I'm still not sure why God would allow something like this to happen, particularly on the morning when a church was saying, "Hey, God, we trust you with our lives. Do what you want. Surprise us."

I wonder what Kyle had been praying. Maybe he had a lot of questions, like we do. Maybe he had prayed, *God, I've got so many questions for you. I wish we could just sit down for lunch and talk some of this stuff out.*

Well, I imagine he's done that by now. Maybe Kyle knows the answers to all the big, hard questions. I'm a little jealous, because along with the rest of us, I'm still here, still seeing things through human eyes. The clarity of our vision is less than perfect. The answers to our questions are incomplete. Theology is still just our understanding of God.

Kyle talked about this in his book *Understanding God's Will*. Here's what he said:

> No matter who you are or where your theology stands, all people who strive to thoughtfully deal with God and life are forced to live within the tension of God's providence and a chaotic world.[3]

Tension.

That's a good word for how I feel when bad things happen to people who are following Jesus as best they know how. I don't like this tension, but that doesn't make it go away.

Some people would say that God caused Kyle's death. I don't know. I don't really want to believe that. However, at the very least, God *allowed* it to happen — right? I mean, if God is sovereign and all-knowing and in control of everything, he could have stopped it — right? Even that is hard to swallow. So here I am stuck in this theological tension, wanting to understand God, but knowing that my understanding is only partial, at best.

What I do know is that we asked God to surprise us that morning. And I had come to Kyle's church hoping to Be the Surprise by bringing a life-changing spiritual experiment to the congregation. Maybe being the hands and feet of Jesus in times like this is as simple as loving those who have been dumped on. Maybe it's just being a friend. Being there. Staying present with people who are being pulled apart by the tension.

For Kyle, the tension is gone, but you and I are still immersed in it. Since we can't eliminate it, we need to learn to be okay with it, to not demand to understand everything, to humbly conclude that living life is far greater than understanding life. *Trusting* God trumps *understanding* God. The train will have long left the station and left us on the platform if we determine to ride only with full understanding. Life will have passed us by. I'm choosing to trust the conductor and the track he's laid down for me.

Kyle never got to deliver his sermon that day, but here is the last line, taken from the script of that last sermon.

Love God, embrace beauty, and live life to the fullest.

Unlike Kyle, you and I have some traveling left to do, some living left to live. Let's board the train with all of our baggage and questions, and live fully, knowing that amid the uncertainty we are loved, we are treasured, and our destination is sure.

21

BURNING BUSHES

About a month after Kyle Lake's death, I got an e-mail from a guy, saying he and two of his buddies wanted to take me to lunch and talk about my book, *Surprise Me*. These guys were casual friends of mine, and I thought, *Great, this will be fun.* We set a lunch date about two weeks out.

But as the day approached, I began wondering about the agenda for the meeting because one of the guys was sending me e-mails with articles and quotes, letting me know that he did not appreciate my theology one little bit. Normally, that wouldn't be a problem.

But what I haven't told you is that after Kyle's death, and the subsequent news stories connecting *Surprise Me* to his death, I started getting scads of hate e-mail from people whose understanding of God differs from mine. One even said, "You should be the dead guy. Too bad you weren't electrocuted with Kyle." Most of these e-mails were either unsigned, or tagged with a postscript that said, "Defending the faith" or "For the cause of Christ."

Now, I'm sure my theology is off in some areas. Whose isn't? He's God — we aren't. What are the odds that any of us have God completely figured out? But based on the e-mails I've received, a number of people seem to think they have.

The far-right leaners said that asking God to surprise us is equivalent to thumbing our noses at God, demanding that he jump through hoops to prove himself with amazing signs and wonders. I tried to tell them that I was asking God to create hoops of *his* choosing, and that I was trying my best to jump through them. They didn't want to have that discussion.

The three guys wanting to meet with me were in the left-leaner's camp. You'll find out what they believe in a moment.

Anyway, unknown to me, Mary had taken the protective measure of getting to my computer before me on some days and deleting the more vitriolic stuff. So as we had breakfast that morning, she said, "You don't need to go to this lunch, you know. Cancel it. Don't put yourself through this."

I almost did. The night before our lunch, the guy had sent me an e-mail that said, "If you want to bring backup, feel free." Not a good sign, but before I left to meet with them, I decided to take Bailey for a walk and ask God what he thought.

Now, you should know that after I realized what this lunch was going to be about, I had taken some time to put together some arguments . . . three pages worth, single-spaced. I had ammo. I was prepared to go to that lunch, guns blazing.

So as I'm walking Bailey, pray-ing, asking God what he wanted me to do, I get a perplexing reply from him. I didn't hear a voice, but it was almost that clear. God said, "Well, Terry, the *last* thing I want you to do today is to argue with these guys."

Huh? That confused me. He continued, "I only have one request of you for this lunch meeting. One. I want you to leave that meeting caring more for these guys than when you came. If you do that, you will have accomplished everything I have asked you to do."

That was it. End of message.

My first reaction was, "Oh, come on, God! I want to argue. I've got some good material here — three pages, single-spaced — from *your* Bible! Let me have at them!"

Silence. Evidently God had already said all he wanted to say.

I told God I would try his approach . . . first. But I wasn't making any promises. If backed into a tight corner, I might let the sheets fly.

So I met the guys at Sunsets in Wayzata. We were seated at our table, and about twenty-eight seconds later, one of them spread a pile of his meticulously prepared ammo across the table, looked up at me, and said, "Fifty-three thousand people leave the church every year, and we believe it's predominantly because of people like you."

Okay. Where did I put my sheets? Where's my Uzi filled with hollow-point bullets packed with Bible references?

I left my sheets in my portfolio, begrudgingly. We talked for two hours. I mostly listened as they told how the Surprise Me experiment — encouraging people to look for God's involvement in their days — would lead people down a path of spiritual disillusionment, because God doesn't intervene in our daily lives any more. According to them, our lives and existences are solely a product of our choices and chance; the Bible is "accurate," but ever since the time of Jesus, God has chosen *not* to actively intervene with us in any way.

I expressed my disagreement with that view and shared a few Scripture quotes. Surprisingly enough, I didn't feel defensive. I didn't get angry. And for the most part, I still cared about these guys by the end of our lunch. Whether I cared *more* . . . well, I'm not sure about that.

As we were wrapping up, agreeing to disagree, a woman walked up to our table. Evidently she had been sitting at the table behind us and had overheard some of our conversation. She said, "Excuse me, but I couldn't help hearing some of what you were saying — I heard you talking about God and stuff. Well, I need help. My husband came home last night and said he wants a divorce. He kicked me out of the house, took my car, my kids, my cell phone . . . I don't know what to do. I came here to lunch today to think, to figure out what to do. I heard you talking about God and thought maybe you could help . . ."

You could see the exhaustion in her face, the sadness and hopelessness. She seemed almost numb.

There was a momentary pause when she finished, then my lunch partners all stood, as if in unison. One said, "Well, this guy wrote a book about stuff like this, so talk to him." And then they walked out. (In all fairness, one of the three had left a few minutes earlier to catch a meeting.)

Elizabeth Barrett Browning wrote, "Earth is crammed with heaven, and every bush afire with God." If God no longer sets bushes on fire, then this woman, Abby, was nothing more than a coincidence. If God no longer intervenes in the lives of humans, then this all happened by chance.

I had quoted the "burning bush" line during lunch and

said, "I'm convinced God still sets bushes on fire, far more often than we think. Maybe our problem is that we're looking for the wrong kinds of bushes. Most burning bushes I see look suspiciously human." When Abby walked up to our table, I smelled smoke. I can't interpret that moment as anything other than a miracle. Maybe the rest of the story will help you see that.

Abby and I sat down and talked for another half hour. She told me that at one time she had a faith in God, she had known Jesus, but had let that relationship slide. She said she wanted to reconnect with God but wasn't sure how to go about that with such a messed up life. I tried to encourage her, saying that people like her were God's specialty. And quite frankly, we're all messed up — none of us is much different from her.

She had heard us talking about the Surprise Me experiment, and she said she wanted to do it, that maybe it would help her reconnect with God. I gave her a book, got her phone number, and said I would call her the next day.

Before Abby left, she threw in a little aside, mentioning that she was an alcoholic. I told her that, *coincidentally*, I was supposed to speak at an alcohol recovery group the following evening. I asked if she wanted to go. She said, "Sure."

Now, put this story on hold for a second while I tell you how I, *coincidentally*, ended up speaking at this recovery group. Yeah, I met another burning bush.

One day I got this call from a raspy-voiced woman. She opened with, "Did you know you wrote a recovery book?"

I said, "Excuse me?"

She said, "*Surprise Me*, it's a recovery book. I've been through eleven different programs to get cleaned up and none of them have worked. *This* one is going to!"

I was a little confused, because the thought of *Surprise Me* being a recovery book had never crossed my mind. Then, to make her claim even more unlikely, the woman went on to say that she was an atheist. Her partner had given her my book while she was in jail from her last DUI, and she had read it and was doing the experiment — minus the God part, of course. (This seemed like a trivial exclusion to her. More on that later.)

"But," she said, "I don't want to just do this experiment for myself; I'm part of another recovery program in St. Paul. I want you to come and introduce this idea to the group." I asked her if she had the authority to make that decision. She said no, but that she would get it.

Tookie (I swear that's her name) doesn't mess around.

A week later I got a call from the lead counselor of this group. She said, "Tookie won't shut up about you and this experiment of yours . . . so, will you come speak to our group? I've got to get her off my back." This recovery group is not faith-based, so just having me come in was a bit of a stretch. And to think that it was pushed through by an atheist, an atheist endorsing a faith-based experiment to a non-faith-based group. Weird, huh?

So I showed up. About twenty people or so sitting in this room. I told them how this experiment had come about, and that I thought it would be a wonderful thing for them to do individually.

"Forget that," said Tookie, "we're going to do this together as a group . . . all of us!" I looked over at Rhonda, the person-in-charge of this program. Then I looked back at Tookie, the person-temporarily-*running* the program, and said, "Okay, here's the plan. I'm going to come back here for the next four Thursday nights. We're all going to do this thing together. See you next Thursday."

I came back the next Thursday. We sat in a big circle. Most of the people in the program were wearing ankle bracelets. Many of them had the tough choice of spending time in jail or enrolling in this program. Hmm? There were people of many faiths, and some with no faith, but they all wanted to do the experiment; they all seemed to sense that they needed something, and they were open to *this* being that something.

That meeting seemed more like church than any church I've ever been in. The room was filled with people who knew they had messed up and weren't trying to act otherwise — they oozed brokenness and humility. I wondered if this was one of the reasons Jesus had chosen to hang out with people who *knew* they were sinners. No cover-up, no down-playing, no rationalizing, no excuses. Just a liberating sense of authenticity.

At the end of that evening, Tookie made one of her classic statements. She said, "Okay, so you're all getting a feel for Terry and his religion. He's kind of into the whole God thing. Me, not so much. I don't believe in God. So, when I do this experiment, I get up in the morning and just say Surprise Me _____, no 'God' at the end. And you can do that too."

I told Tookie thanks for weighing in on that one, and we dismissed till the next week.

On the following Thursday, I came back, but this time I had Abby, the woman from the restaurant, with me. She had already started doing the experiment and had written several pages in her journal. She read some of it that night and told her story of how we had met.

The group was touched by her story, and they added some amazing insights of their own. There were plenty of tears and stories of finding God in the ordinary moments of their days. At the end of the evening, Tookie cleared her throat and said, "Well, you might as well know — I've started praying Surprise Me *god* . . . but it's with a *little* 'g'!"

I smiled at her.

The next week the group began referring to themselves as "the chosen caught." In other words, they felt they were chosen by God to get caught, so that they could then go out and help others who were struggling with alcohol. Pretty amazing, huh?

By week four, I was sorry to have to wrap up the experiment. I didn't want to leave this group. This month had done at least as much for me as it had for the recovery group. The highlight of the night for me was when Tookie, softened from the previous month, seemed to undig her heels a bit. She told us, "I just want you all to know something . . . the 'G' is getting bigger."

The "G" is getting bigger.

Wow. That's a faith statement if I've ever heard one.

If I can spend my life doing things that, when observed by others, grows the "G" in their lives, then I will have spent my time and energy well.

By the end of the month Abby was a changed person. Tookie was changed. I was changed. Many people in the recovery program were changed. Wherever our "Gs" had started the month, they were chubbier by the end. And that's all God's looking for, for us to have a relationship with him that is moving forward, becoming more intimate, more real, more healthy.

The three guys I met with at the restaurant? I haven't spoken to two of them since that day. One of them sent me a short e-mail a while back saying, "STOP WHAT YOU ARE DOING, IMMEDIATELY!!!!!!!!!!" Yes, it was all caps and he actually had about eighteen exclamation marks. I still would like to talk with these guys some more. I do care about them. I'm not angry with them, at all. I've actually asked God if he wants me to pursue them. No answer so far. That story needs an ending yet.

So let's recap, let's follow the illogical trail of burning bushes in these stories.

Kyle Lake dies.

E-mails start pouring in from critics. Fan mail!

Three guys hear about it and set up lunch.

God tells me not to argue, but to love. Bummer.

Abby (aka The Burning Bush) comes up to our table.

She tells me she's an alcoholic.

Tookie, an alcoholic, calls me.

Tookie becomes a pest to her counselor.

Her counselor schedules me to speak to the group. (To get an atheistic burning bush named Tookie off her back. Note — God sets atheists on fire, just so he can put them out.)

Abby comes to the recovery group.

Shares her story.

Whole group does experiment.

Tookie: "The 'G' is getting bigger."

If each of Abby and Tookie resembled a burning bush, then each of them also required a response. Each bush needed someone to care, to throw water on the bush — to put out the fire, to listen, to help, to love.

We'll never Be the Surprise if we don't recognize the flaming shrubs in our lives, and we'll never Be the Surprise if we walk away from those shrubs. God entrusts us with the power to encourage others, to quench his burning bushes, to water them, love them. But we can't walk away. We have to engage.

Jesus said, "If you love me, you will keep my commandments."

One of his commands is, "Love your neighbor as yourself."

Be . . . the . . . Surprise.

EVERYTHING IS HOLY NOW

*When I was a boy, each week
On Sunday, we would go to church
And pay attention to the priest
As he would read the Holy Word.
And consecrate the holy bread
And everyone would kneel and bow
Today the only difference is
Everything is holy now.
Everything, everything,
Everything is holy now . . .*

*When I was in Sunday school
We would learn about the time
Moses split the sea in two
Jesus made the water wine*

And I remember feeling sad
That miracles don't happen still
But now I can't keep track
'Cause everything's a miracle
Everything, everything
Everything's a miracle . . .

Wine from water is not so small
But an even better magic trick
Is that anything is here at all
So the challenging thing becomes
Not to look for miracles
But finding where there isn't one

When holy water was rare at best
Barely wet my fingertips
Now I have to hold my breath
Like I'm swimming in a sea of it
It used to be world half there
Heaven's second rate hand-me-down
But I'm walking with a reverent air
'Cause everything is holy now

Read a questioning child's face
To say it's not a testament
That'd be very hard to say
See another new morning come
To say it's not a sacrament
I'd tell you that it can't be done

This morning outside I stood
And saw a little red-winged bird
Shining like a burning bush
Singing like a scripture verse
It made me want to bow my head
And pray without a sound
How things have changed since then
Everything is holy now

Everything, everything
Everything is holy now
Everything, everything,
Everything is holy now

23

SUNSETS & TRAFFIC JAMS

I usually don't ride my bicycle to Taylor's soccer games because there's something about me, her dad, in spandex that is off-putting to her. But this day I did. I rode to the soccer field, hopped off my bike, and started watching the game.

Cheryl Desantis came up to me and said, "Okay, you're just the person I need to talk to." She proceeded to tell me how she wanted Gary, her husband, to have more downtime — relaxing, having fun, hanging out with friends. So on Father's Day, she bought him a brand-new bicycle. Not just any old bike, but a Trek OCLV 120 carbon fiber frame with Mavic Ksyrium racing wheels and Shimano Ultegra componentry. For the uninitiated in the crowd, what that means is, it wasn't cheap.

She went on to tell me how Gary was planning on returning the bike because it was too expensive and he just didn't need one that nice. She told me she wanted him to have it; she wanted him to have a fast bike because Gary doesn't do "slow."

I got his cell number from her, called him, right there on

the sidelines of the soccer field, and asked him to drive by the game. I said, "Your wife wants me to have a chat with you." He came by. I explained the finer points of this addictive hobby and this speed machine he had in his possession and, well, he bought it ... Zipp wheels, titanium cassette, and derailleur. Oh, how he bought it. Since then we've biked thousands of miles together.

Fast-forward a few years. . . . Four of us cycling addicts went on a training trip to Arizona. Gary has a place down there and we make an annual trip every February — four middle-aged men doing their very best Lance Armstrong impersonations. Sure, we're pathetic, but we don't care.

One of our rides was a switchback climb from Sedona up to Flagstaff. We drove to Sedona in the morning, made the ride, hopped back in the van, and headed home to Phoenix. On the way back, we hit the largest traffic snag I've ever seen in my life. Interstate 17 was shut down — not stop and go, stopped/ closed/going nowhere. For a stretch of twenty-five miles, the freeway was a parking lot with cars bumper to bumper — engines shut off, nobody moving. Trapped.

Now, this could have been stressful; people could have been angry, yelling, screaming, honking . . . but just the opposite happened. I wouldn't have believed it if I hadn't been there and seen it for myself.

This event initiated my all-time favorite bike ride with Gary. We opened the back of the van, pulled out our bikes, and proceeded to ride down the middle of I-17 in broad daylight, weaving in and out of the parked cars as if we ruled the asphalt — kings of the road. It was heaven. Cyclists finally had all the power. If I would have had a horn, I would have laid on that thing. "Move it, cars!" People even offered to trade their cars for our bikes.

We headed toward the front-end of the traffic jam, but we never got there. As we rode down the middle of a three-lane free-way, we saw parties popping up. All over the place. Guys in a pickup were grilling brats from their truck bed with the music pumping in the cab. Two other guys were giving an impromptu guitar concert while sitting on the bumper of their car. Frisbees were flying. Parents were pushing babies down I-17 in strollers. Gary stopped to make the acquaintance of some of these babies and to tickle a chin or two.

Our bike ride, which had started as a trip to discover the source of the traffic problem, had now become a bike ride about, well, the ride. We almost forgot where we were going because the process of getting there was much more fun. When we turned around and headed back, I found myself thanking God for putting on the brakes to life, if only for a few hours.

My joy was dented a bit when someone who had seen us pass, going the other way, asked, "Did you get to the front? Did you see the accident? We heard that a girl didn't make it, is that true?"

Whoa. Someone had paid a pretty high price to give us this slice of life that we just lived. It seemed unfair that we were benefiting, in a strange sort of way, from this girl's tragedy. But then I realized that when sacrifices pave the way for life-giving gifts, it would be wrong to not accept those gifts, to appreciate them, to open them.

We were almost back to the car when we noticed people

heading to the western edge of the highway. The attraction was one of the most beautiful sunsets I've ever seen. Chunks of purple and orange and pink. People who had been in a raging hurry several hours ago stood in peaceful silence, watching till the sun dropped over the foothills.

I secretly wondered if this sunset was for the girl at the front of the line. Maybe life is a twenty-five mile line, a big traffic jam of sorts. Someday, sooner or later, we all end up at the front of the line. It's our turn. And we don't really know when that will be. . . . I don't think we come to the front of the line as much as the front of the line comes to us. It's a deceptive inevitability.

A couple days after we returned from our trip, Gary's wife, Cheryl, ended up at the front of the line. She died unexpectedly, suddenly, in a bizarre set of health circumstances that nobody saw coming. It was devastating, as it always is when the front of the line arrives without warning.

But Cheryl was ready. She had traveled her twenty-five miles on I-17 and tasted the brats and listened to the music and thrown a Frisbee and tickled the chins of babies — and cherished her friends and loved her children and married her high-school sweetheart and looked in the face of God and said, "If this is the front of the line, show me what's on the other side."

I think the sunset *was* for the girl at the front of the line. And from the other side, where Cheryl now stands with her Creator, she knows that the last sunset is really just the first sunrise.

§ § §

I-17 is the present. It's all we have, right now.

Gary and I could have left our bikes in the car and sat out

the traffic jam, but we would have missed the brats, the babies, the music . . . the beauty. We would have missed a perspective-changing three hours of our lives. In the same way, I made a *present* choice that allowed me to meet Gary for the first time. I didn't know him before that soccer game, but because I broke the "rule" and showed up at my daughter's game on my bike (in spandex), his wife saw me, and because she saw me on a bike, she asked me to convince Gary to keep the bike that she had bought for him. Because I called him on the spot, Gary came, he rode, he got hooked, and because he got hooked, he was welcomed into a new circle of friends, a community that is helping him through this painful time in his life.

So often we view the present as merely transitional — the moment we have to get past in order to get to where we really want to go. The thing is, where we "really want to go" isn't here yet, and the present may never allow us to get there. Our I-17 might take us in a totally different direction.

I also think that skimming over the present to experience the future indicates a certain arrogance. It says, "I know the future, I know where I'm going, so I'm going to circumvent the present to expedite my arrival there." Sure, it's good to plan ahead, but if we forego the present in favor of the future, we may be trading the only thing we have for something that will never be.

Cheryl didn't know the future would be so short. Neither did Kyle Lake. He was only thirty-three. He thought there were miles left on his I-17.

Both Cheryl and Kyle were the kind of people who tasted the brats, threw the Frisbee, listened to the music, tickled the chins of babies — loved their families, their friends, and their

God. All of this they did in the present. They got everything out of their I-17 that it had to offer.

Every day we wake up on the on-ramp of *our* I-17. Two cups of Joe and we're up to speed, merging onto the right lane of the expressway called Today. But wait; there's a hitchhiker on the on-ramp. Do you see him? He's easy to miss sometimes because he's not holding a sign or anything. That's God. He is saying, "I'd like to go along with you for the ride today. Have you got room?"

The present will never reveal its full potential unless God is riding with us, enhancing our awareness of it. God brings the present to life, or should I say he brings life to the present. When we live with this awareness, we will no longer desire to rush past the *now*, hoping that our *later* will be better, because the *now* will have become our favorite stretch of highway.

Before you merge into Today, consider picking up that understated hitchhiker sitting to the side of the on-ramp.

24

DOMESTIQUES

I went on a brutal bike ride today with my friends Gary and Ed. We did about thirty miles into a thirty miles per hour headwind. Those "thirties" almost cancelled each other out. We were pedaling hard, but making marginal headway. It was like trying to ride through a wall.

Gary and I tried to create a draft for Ed since he is new to cycling. We always say that new riders get a free one-year, no-pulling pass. The front guy in the line, the one doing the hardest work, is considered the puller. He's "taking a pull," and everybody else in line is "on the couch" or "wheel-sucking." Drafting.

Ed was tucked in about six inches off our back wheels. Because we were pulling him, he was able to maintain his speed, yet save about 30 to 40 percent of his energy output.

When racing, I don't want people wheel-sucking off of me, because it means they are resting and recovering while I'm busting my butt. It means when a sprint happens, I'll be 80 percent spent and they'll be fresh. It means I'll get dropped. It means I'll lose.

Now, if the wheel-sucker is a teammate, that's different.

Often in cycling there are teammates whose job it is to pull, to protect the best rider or sprinter on the team so that when it comes to the end of the race, he will be fresh and have the energy to power through that last sprint and win. Those work-horses, often called domestiques, sacrifice their chances of winning for someone else, for the team.

Sorry, I didn't intend for this to be Cycling 101.

But cycling has some interesting parallels with this experiment. In order for me to Be the Surprise for someone else, I have to be willing to pull. I have to be willing to sacrifice my wishes, my desires, and my agenda for the sake of someone else.

I'm not saying that in order to Be the Surprise you *always* have to be the domestique, but you must always be *willing* to be the domestique. If the team captain, the Directeur Sportif, asks you to pull, you pull.

Jesus set the tone for this when he said, "The last will be first, and the first will be last" (Matthew 20:16, NIV). And "So you want first place? Then take the last place. Be the servant of all" (Mark 9:35).

Not every cyclist is a good sprinter. Not every cyclist is a good climber. Not many of us can win the race, but we might be perfectly suited to help one of our teammates win. We might just be the perfect domestique. Maybe we were designed for that very role.

When Jesus said, "[I] did not come to be served, but to serve" (Mark 10:45, NIV), he was saying, "I came to work for your good. Hop in my draft, and I'll take you to the finish line."

A domestique helps others win.

A domestique helps others feel valued, cared for, and loved.

Here's the rub. Becoming a domestique is hard. None of us come to this role naturally, and I am no exception. Learning to serve comes through a process not unlike death, the death of our desires to be viewed as the best, the fastest, the smartest, the prettiest, the coolest, the richest, the most famous — the winner of the stinkin' Tour de France. (Let it go, Terry!)

One of my other cycling buddies is a great domestique. A natural. Tom Garlinghouse. I lovingly refer to him as the Garlington Northern because when I get in his draft, it's like being pulled along by a locomotive. It doesn't hurt that Tom is 6' 4" and two hundred pounds. He tames the wind with his frame, and when I am tucked in behind him, I am truly "on the couch."

The Garlington Northern is also a more natural *spiritual* domestique than I. Tom has a knack for reaching down to people and pulling them up. Serving others seems intuitive for him. Caring and kindness swirl in his wake, making light loads for those in close proximity to him. He does it not just for others, but also for God. Joyfully. I respect that about him. He hasn't helped me win any races, but he has helped me through some tough days.

Can I do my pulling as a gift to God, not just for Ed? Can I be like Brother Lawrence and peel potatoes and clean bathrooms as an offering to God? Could I bus tables for God, like Wilma?

Being the Surprise is about being willing to pull. Even when it hurts.

Gary, Ed, and I turned back east, felt the wind swing around to our backs, and went from fifteen miles per hour to thirty-five miles per hour. Yeah, baby! We flew. No pulling necessary; we were drafting the wind itself.

We pulled into our favorite little coffee shop called Retro Roast, just on the edge of Loretto. They've got the best green tea smoothies in the world. We've gotten acclimated to these smoothies, so our bikes almost instinctively head to Retro. When I get on my bike, making that first pedal stroke, I can sometimes almost taste the smoothie. Pavlovian.

Three guys, exhausted, sucking down smoothies.

Three guys who beat back the wind, and then rode it.

Three guys who have pulled, and will continue to pull, for each other.

Three happy domestiques.

25

A SIMPLE TOUCH

Tookie recently showed me an essay she had written. She didn't know I was writing a book about being the fingers and toes of Jesus, but I'd say this fits in pretty well. Check it out.

Say It[4]

By Tookie

I caught kindness red-handed the other day.

Waiting for a bus, any old bus, on the corner of 8th and Nicollet on Monday, any old Monday, I noticed two African-American teenage boys in need of attention.

Their caps sideways, their blue jeans sunk to unforgettable depths, the blinding whites of their new sneakers contrasting with their black, black hair. They were having fun, high-fiving each other. Fancy fives: low fives, high fives, behind-the-back fives, between-the-legs fives — any old fives — creating raucous laughter and high-pitched squeals. Their silliness was infectious.

The any-old bus stopped at the corner and before passengers had a chance to debus, the two slammed into the open entrance causing chaos and outright anger from tired Monday-night commuters.

"Well," I thought, "This will be an interesting ride."

I jammed into the overcrowded bus and noticed the two boys had been separated. I was relieved. One found an empty seat toward the rear; the other sat in a handicapped seat close to the front, close to me. So close, in fact, I began to count his beautiful eyelashes and trace the perfect contour of his brow. But he was scowling.

Almost as if he expected aisle-standing bus riders to step on his feet, brush his hands with their clothing, or in some way invade his space, he curled himself into a defensive ball. Waiting. Waiting for trouble. Scowling.

"People, please move back as far as you can," announced the large bus driver, with authority in her voice. Like sheep, the passengers complied, giving space to those sardined in front, in front of the boy with the scowl. I measured his chest as he silently sighed with relief. I caught myself breathing for him.

The bus lumbered on to the next stop. Standers stumbled and swayed, anticipating the worst as they braced for the inevitable block-to-block stop.

Someone dropped an apple that found its way to the front steps. I saw the boy's face change as the Red Delicious tumbled down the aisle. He caught me looking at him as he, like a child discovering a new animal, wanted to point and name and puff with pride. For a second he forgot. For a second, he wanted to be sure someone else saw and smiled.

Like liquid moving from beaker to beaker, the bus filled and emptied, emptied and filled with new faces, different smells. An elderly woman struggled to board the bus' steep steps, and I watch him watch her. By the time the woman paid her fare and turned to face the swollen bus, the boy had jumped up and wordlessly offered his seat. Expectantly she sat. Unappreciatively she brooded.

The door closed; the bus picked up speed. The boy stood next to my seat now and I could smell his cologne. I nudged him and said, "That was very nice of you."

He didn't hear me so he leaned down, trusting his instincts for tone and body language, yet on alert, he said, "What?"

I repeated, exactly, "That was very nice of you."

He straightened, took a step sideways, and I could see, even though most of his face was turned away from me, the whitest, widest smile flash across his face.

For three city blocks I thought his teeth were going to dry out. When my bus corner approached and he saw me prepare for departure, he turned, full-faced, and said to me, "You have a nice day, lady, ya know? And thank you."

Sometimes all you have to do is — say it.

Profound.

I still see Tookie. We have breakfast, talk on the phone. She's become a good friend. Her brain is about as nonlinear as mine, so we entertain and confuse each other.

The size of her "G" is sporadic; some days it's bigger and healthier than others. Of course, we could all probably say that.

I've realized that it's not my job to measure Tookie's "G," or to make judgments on the spiritual pie chart of my friends. My job is to *be* their friend — regardless of their current position on the spiritual-depth continuum. Fingers and toes don't judge, they just do the work they find before them.

They touch.

All I know is that Tookie's comment to this boy carried the touch of "G" . . . a fairly good-sized "G."

26

WWF — WRESTLING WITH FAITH

Wrestling with our faith may seem an undesirable activity, but it's not. It's a necessary staple of our spiritual life. It's necessary even for those who don't have a faith because in order for them to arrive at the conclusion that faith and God don't exist, they have to wrestle with the possibility of God's existence.

I'm learning to thoroughly enjoy this hand-to-hand combat of sorts. It's the one activity where I feel most alive, most real. When locking arms and minds with God, I am sampling, testing, and tasting what life is really about. I am exploring who I am and who he is, and how this odd couple fits together to form something creative and purposeful. My wrestling helps me to *be*, which in turn helps me to *do* for others.

The following is a sampling of some of that wrestling — a short excerpt of a dialogue between a guy named Brian and myself.

Terry,

It's been awhile since we've chatted.

My life has been crazy this past year. Two hospital stays, one appendectomy, and the preparation for our first child, due in late December-early January. Yes, it's been a busy year. I have been thinking of contacting you in regard to your *Surprise Me* book.

Just as a brief picture of where I'm coming from: Heidi and I left the church a year ago last April. We didn't leave in anger, we just were asking questions that didn't have a place in the church. Since then we've been on a journey. I have been reading a lot of writings by Catholic mystics and Buddhist monks, along with tons of other stuff. I have been willing to take on the "label" mystic. And with that hat firmly in place, I have found myself pondering your book. I feel it's an invitation into a mystic practice. To me, asking God to surprise you on a daily basis is like asking God to give you a mystical experience.

Over a year ago when I did the Surprise Me experiment, I failed after 15 days. I didn't fail because I slacked off; I didn't fail because I lost interest; I failed because I could not handle the things I saw when God surprised me. I wasn't the person that I am today.

It's as if I was standing on a huge iceberg and reaching up to God, saying, "All of this ice is not mine. It's ice I was told to believe without knowing the reasons to believe it. It's too hard to melt all of this ice on my own. I need you, God, to melt it for me." And in the middle of the Surprise Me experiment that is exactly what happened. The ice melted and I was suddenly drowning in the water. What was Truth? I was lost. I know it is only by the grasp of God that I was kept from drowning in that pool. But I didn't know that then, and it was a scary experience.

Would others have this same experience, I wonder? If people are really looking for God to reveal Himself in their daily lives, it might be more than they are ready for. I know that people who really open themselves up the way I think you want them to will be in for something amazing. But will they grab tight to the hand of God, or panic in the rush of water? I don't know. I'm probably way off base. That's probably the reason I haven't written you until now. But I had to get it off my chest.
Brian

Hey Brian,

Thanks for the great e-mail. I think you're dead-on. And more and more I consider myself a mystic as well. I'm reading some of the same stuff and enjoying it thoroughly.

Yeah, engaging in a spiritual experiment

like Surprise Me, when done with an honest heart that is truly searching, will melt icebergs. Yeah, it's dangerous. Yeah, it will cause a flood. Yeah, it will rock people's religious boats to the point of taking on water. But I would rather we all drown in honest searching, than that we all freeze our apathetic rear ends on Stepford religion. Is faith-on-ice real faith? I don't think so.

Plus, I believe God's heart and desire for us is to question and wrestle and doubt, and maybe even gulp in some water and lose our breath. I don't think he wants us chilling; he wants us flailing away, fighting for every ounce of truth we can grasp. And I believe he honors that flailing.

Will some people drown in their questions and walk away from faith — and God? Maybe. Probably. But what kind of faith are they walking away from? Was it real? Was it worth hanging on to? Was it ever even capable of creating spiritual buoyancy? Or was it just a waterlogged board that looked like it could float, but never really did? It looked like faith but was fake. If they lose their grip on that, what have they lost? Maybe it's just the motivation they need to swim on, looking for the real relationship with God.

I think that sometimes we need to go down a few times before we can come up. Maybe that's the trouble with religion in America.

We're dog-paddling water-treaders who are convinced that buoyancy is internally manufactured, that it's *our* efforts that keep us afloat.

Trust, at the very least, requires the willingness to stop paddling and to go down. Then, when God blows wind into our lungs, we resurface and realize that drowning is not our biggest danger, but rather treading water. Losing our faith shouldn't worry us . . . but hanging on to a losable faith should.

To you I say, keep flailing. Trust the depths. Doubt all you want . . . all you can. Own it. I believe that God is near, and he's in the process of spiritually oxygenating you, making you into a real live *floater*. Buoyancy is waiting.

Have a great day.

Terry

Terry,

I couldn't agree more. Hanging on to a losable faith should scare us. That statement gets to the very root of the problem with evangelical Christianity in American culture. People just seem to be afraid. They seem afraid that something is going to come along and invalidate everything they believe. And I believe the only thing that could cause such invalidity is the very fear these folks have wrapped themselves up in.

Faith, to me, is like a castle of cards. It's built of something totally fragile. This fragile state is found in the fact that faith is believing in things unseen, unproveable. When fear is your guiding force, you worry constantly about the card castle; you worry that the slightest wind of another faith or idea might knock the castle over. But people with a faith that is without fear see their castles in a different light. I told a friend of mine that I knew I could take a sledgehammer to his card castle of faith, and it would remain standing. As a matter of fact, I think that the sledgehammer might actually break on it. That's Faith.

Confidence in your faith isn't found in how well you protect it, but in how much you believe in it. My castle isn't too big yet. I had a huge castle for a while, but the slightest winds knocked it down. I'm rebuilding, but I'm rebuilding with materials I know will stand those tests of my faith.

So I agree, a faith lived in fear is a faith worth losing.

Your response to my e-mail was enlightening. Keep in touch with what's going on in your head from time to time.

Brian

Brian,

Can I add to/mess with your analogy? I love the card castle thing. I love the idea of taking a sledgehammer to it. It sounds like you've been doing a lot of that in the past year. I wish more Christians wielded sledgehammers. Too many of us are cautiously painting the siding of our card castles with tiny little brushes, trying not to disturb the paper-spined architecture.

I think faith is built by reduction; it's demolished into existence. Isn't it just like God to do things the opposite way that everybody else does them? We don't grasp Truth by adding to it, but by chipping away at it — excavating for it. It's already there, we just have to unearth it and remove the layers of faux truth. When we swing the sledge, it chips away at the two of clubs and the nine of spades. If we swing long and hard enough (the flailing I was talking about earlier) eventually we feel the clunk of our hammer onto something akin to bedrock. We set down the hammer, scrape the rubble away with our fingers, and there standing on end is the ace of hearts, the core we've been looking for. All the castle we need. All the Truth we need. Foundational faith. God alone.

I love your sentence, "Confidence in your faith isn't found in how well you protect it, but in how much you believe in it." I might state it like this — Confidence in your faith can't be undone if it was your undoing that brought you to it. Faith won't break if it was brokenness that formed it.

A truth-seeking sledgehammer will destroy only that which wears the brittle *shell* of Truth. That's why I don't worry about people's faith breaking (or drowning) because of the Surprise Me thing. What crumbles is counterfeit. What's left is real.

Of course this premise is predicated on the fact that the person doing the seeking is really seeking and not just pretending to do so. There are plenty of pretenders out there. Those people *really* confuse me. Why would you pretend to be hungry for a steak if you didn't like meat?

Again, it's fun noodling with you.

Terry

This is an example of what I call constructive wrestling. These discussions, while voicing doubts and questions, help us to work through our doubts and questions. When our questions remain unspoken, we become static in our faith. Stuck. Forward motion ceases, and the longer we sit on questions without voicing them, the more we sink into the religious sludge that restricts our hands and feet.

The result? We're unhappy in our faith, or whatever it is we call faith. We look and feel lethargic, not just spiritually, but also physically.

We can no longer be the hands and feet of Jesus because *being* has ceased. Even when we act from a sense of goodness, it is a dutiful *action*, not a heartfelt *reaction*. This is not a picture of abundant life; this is a picture of a religious life.

So be like Jacob from the Old Testament. Wrestle all night long. Wrestle till dawn. Wrestle till you die . . . or rather, wrestle till you live.

27

CHIPS 'N' CHEESE MESSIAH

Some people think we can figure Jesus out, predict his whereabouts.

They think he is a place — a church, a political leaning, or a particular theology. That he has coordinates of latitude and longitude, an address, a home base where he does his business (whatever that is), and that we can go back to that place and find him. That he will always be right where we left him.

They move Jesus around like a piece on a gameboard, positioning him where *they* want him, so he'll fit into *their* game plan. They try to use him to "jump" their detractors and eliminate contrary thinkers.

They treat Jesus as if he is their personal lap dog. Give him a treat and tell him to "stay." Occasionally they let him run, but only as long as he stays within their invisibly fenced theology. If he strays, well, they have to give him a shock; otherwise, he might get lost, and they would constantly have to go out looking for him. What a hassle that would be.

This Jesus is comfy, cozy, safe, harmless . . . and he's *useless!*

This Jesus is a myth.

This Jesus does not exist.

When our daughter Lauren was little, she had onesie pajamas, you know, the kind with the built-in rubber footies. She loved them. Mary and I loved them. They were easy for us to put on, hard for Lauren to take off, and the built-in rubber-soled feet gave her traction when scooting around the hardwood kitchen floor.

But there was a problem. Lauren was active — in constant motion. We couldn't control her, and she was warm-blooded. She had an excellent heater, and her little toes got sweaty . . . seriously sweaty. After two nights in the jammies, her footies started to smell like a freshly microwaved plate of chips 'n' cheese. Not a good nighttime odor.

Before long we came to the conclusion that in order to stay fresh, locomotion feet like hers need to be free. So we cut the footies off all of her pajamas.

Fresh air. Smell gone. Problem solved.

Jesus wore sandals. This is not coincidental. A static messiah may have been able to get away with footie pajamas. A couch-potato savior may have tolerated rubber-wrapped toes without developing podiatric chips 'n' cheese.

Not Jesus. He scooted around the kitchen floor of Galilee collecting recruits by saying, "*Follow* me." He didn't do "stand up" in a hut and wrap up his daily routine with a "Thank you, thank you. I'll be right here every night." Jesus is more transition than position, more drive than neutral, more river than pond. He's a breeze, a tide, a route, an arc.

Curt Hinkle gave me this idea of a moving Jesus. He says the static messiah is the Jesus of religion; a moving Jesus is for

Christ-*followers*.

Jesus is on the move. We don't know where he's going, so we need to follow him, come to him. Tomorrow we need to come to him again, where he *is*, not where he *was*. To do this, we have to move too. We can't be static if we want to be *with* Jesus. To be with a moving Jesus, we need free feet.

Have you ever caught the scent of chips 'n' cheese around Christians who kneel at the feet of a static Jesus? Grab some scissors, free your toes, and *follow*.

"How blessed the feet of him who *follows* after you."

28

BARRON VON RICKENBACKER

KaBOOM! 4:43 a.m. *Lightning just struck somewhere — close.* That was my first semiconscious thought today. Bailey, our dog, scampered into our room, which she always does after exceptional claps of thunder. She's not allowed into our room, except when she's too petrified to remember the rules and I'm too tired to uphold them. It's a truce observed through fear and apathy.

I have a friend who might as well have been struck by lightning a few years ago. His name is Rick Barron — Rickermortis. (I always feel the need to add some weird suffix to Rick's name. I don't do this with most people, but for some reason, I can't help myself when it comes to Rick.) Rick-atoni is a singer/songwriter/guitar player that I used to hire to sing and play on many of my commercials. I met him right after he moved back from Los Angeles, where he had a publishing deal to spend his days writing songs for Warner Chapel. Tough gig.

Rick has always been a curious spiritual soul. Tons of questions, tons of doubts, but always eager to explore. Over the years we've discussed the big questions — God, life, faith, death — and even though Rick humors me most of the time, underneath it all he is thinking, formulating a belief system, constructing a faith.

Late one night he stopped to help someone along the highway who had just had a car accident. Rick parked on the shoulder and walked over to help. He was just getting to this car when a drunk driver plowed into that car, which then plowed into Rick. My friend took a major hit to the midsection. Lots of internal bleeding. Stomach, intestines, kidneys rearranged. It took a map, mesh, and duct tape to reassemble Rick's disassembled organs and hold them in their rightful place.

Over the years I had given Rick a few books to read and offered to discuss them with him. He always found a way to push it off.

That night on my way to the hospital to visit him, I felt nudged to buy him a Bible. This is not normal for me. Typically, I'm not an overzealous dispenser of Bibles, but I stopped in at a local bookstore and picked one up for him. I was wondering if this was it — the end of the road for Rick, or maybe the end of his career. Anyhow, I wrote some stuff in the Bible and headed to visit him.

When I walked into his room, Rick was still unconscious. I stood for a long time, just looking at him. Had he ever really heard me? Did he know I cared about him, that God cared about him? I told God it would be a terrible waste to lose Rick. He's too stinking talented.

I put the Bible down on the tray and left.

I don't know what happened or how, but somehow Rick

survived, not just physically, but spiritually. God found him in that room. Rick came out of the hospital like a cannon shot.

Since that day, Rick has been: (1) on tour with Jonny Lang as a back-up singer and guitar player, (2) on a USA tour of his own as a solo artist, and (3) the musical director at a church. (He's about as likely a choice for church worship leader as Larry the Cable Guy is for a marriage counselor/yoga instructor. Not that Rick isn't qualified; it's just that he might be too qualified. He knows R&B and funk and reggae and blues and . . . you know, all those styles of music you love but have never, ever, ever, ever, ever heard in a church. Well, there's a church in Brooklyn Park, Minnesota, that's hearing it now.)

Rick used to talk about wanting that one big hit, that million-dollar, number-one single. Now he talks about wanting to make a difference, to love people and help them to find the source of that love. Money is never part of the discussion.

Last week I went to Bunkers, a local music hole, with Rick, Joe, and Craig T. A local band, Dr. Mambo's Combo, was playing that night, but Rick had learned that Jonny Lang was going to drop by and sit in. Who doesn't want to see Jonny Lang go off on his guitar in a small club?

When we arrived around ten, the place was packed with musicians and players from the local music scene. Evidently we weren't the only ones privy to the top-secret info about Jonny's appearance. As I waded through the crowd to a table, I kept running into old friends, musicians and singers I had worked with over the years. It was a reunion of sorts. J. D. Steele, Mark Licktieg, Tommy Barbarella, Bill Brown, Billy Franze, Margaret Cox, Michael Bland, Dave Barry . . . these people have played with everyone from Prince to Janet

Jackson. They have sung and performed on TV commercials you would recognize — you could sing.

It was one of those rare nights of musical perfection. It seemed like God was showing off, showing off his chops through his creatures. The Combo was the *announced* band tonight, but the stage shuffled with players every time someone noticed another all-star in the crowd. These musicians hadn't practiced together, but it didn't matter. They all had been divinely injected with uber-talent to the point it just oozed out through Fenders and Zildians and Wurlitzers to the tune of about 110 decibels.

Bill and Tommy B tag-teamed the Hammond B3, almost making it beg for mercy. Mark poured so much soul into his vocals that it made you wonder first, *Is he really white?* and second, *How do you not have a cardiac arrest when you put that much heart into your vocals?*

It was art, the great art of God. Creativity raged across that stage. Michael Bland's funkified rock-tight grooves and fills came straight out of heaven. And the big finale? Billy F. and Jonny — a dueling guitars "lick off." No band, no back up, just two guys who speak better through frets and strings, trading licks. Billy leading and Jonny copping it, for about ten minutes. When Billy did a long riff that would have lost Stevie Ray, Jonny burst out laughing.

Somewhere in the middle of all this, Rick leaned over to me and said, "Do you know what I see here tonight? I see a garden — a garden that you and I have had the privilege of watering."

Then he said, "You know, Terry, if you hadn't brought me that Bible in the hospital, many of these people would not have been watered, because I would have had no water to give them." We didn't talk about it anymore that evening, but I enjoyed the music in an even more profound way for the rest of the night.

(Chronological pause.)

It's now about two months later. I'm sitting on the balcony of a hotel room in Puerto Vallarta. My wife and our daughter Taylor are down at the pool, basking in UV and umbrella drinks, and I'm sitting here with my laptop, trying to polish off the initial draft of this book before deadline. As I look out over the palm trees, feeling sorry for myself (cue pseudo-sympathy strings), my BlackBerry buzzes, telling me I have a new e-mail.

Since the steel drum music has already put my focus in "hang loose" mode, I pick it up and see it's an e-mail from Rick. Hmm. Here's what it said.

> How's it going Gilbert? (He loves to torture me with my middle name.)
>
> Miss you man. Get *Be the Surprise* done and come hang out with me.

He went on — and caught me by surprise with his words.

> I'm glad God picked a mutt like you to deliver a bone like Him to a starving mutt like me. Thanks for sharing His bone with me, Terry. His bone has held me up through these last nine years through times where I'm sure my

bones would have collapsed and broken. You gave me the best gift a person can give another person. You gave me Him.

Now, come with me on an adventure, my friend. Suspend reality for a minute will you? . . .

It's forty years from now . . . you're lying in a bed, dying. Mary and your kids and grand-kids are by your side. You start to feel afraid. You become aware there are angels in the room. Somehow their presence calms you.

Mary holds your hand and says, "It's okay, honey. It's okay, just let go. I'll be there with you before you know it." Your eyes are closed. They have been for three days now. But you hear everything—the whirring of the machines, the drip of the IV, your kids in the back of the room, crying. You hear a voice, far off in the distance, call your name.

You feel a strange, divisive pull in your heart. A need to stay. A need to go.

Why is it getting so hard to breathe? You feel a pressure building, in your chest, behind your eyes. *What is happening to me?*

You see a beautiful light off in the distance and start the long walk toward it . . . the dull pain and the need to breathe fade into the dis-tance. You're running now. How long has it been since you've run? You look down at your legs and they look different somehow, younger.

You sprint toward the light, smiling, light as a feather. A thought occurs to you, *Where was I just a minute ago?*

The light is getting closer, closer, closer.

Up ahead you see a slide with a long line of people waiting to go down it. You join them and wait, for what could be seconds or years. Suddenly you are at the front of the line. You settle into the slide, grab hold of the rails, and pull . . . and then . . . you're free. At that very moment you realize you made the right choice. It's all true. Every word. He does exist. He does keep His promises.

Back on earth, your body, with you no longer in it, sits, propped up straight in bed, your vacant eyes stare off into somewhere far, far away. Your lungs draw one last great breath. Your empty body deflates like a dime store balloon.

The slide ends in front of two impossibly enormous doors. They swing open for you. Curious, you step inside.

A voice calls to you from the back of a beautiful cathedral; it is far beyond your imagination's picture of big. You hear the most heavenly music coming from, well, everywhere. The voice says, "Well done my good and faithful servant, I am well-pleased with you. You finished the race. The prize is yours. Welcome to heaven, my beloved son, Terry."

All the years of not enough time, or money, or faith. Gone. You do not feel the need to look backwards anymore. There is no more past. Only future.

The voice booms across the vastness around you. "Whom here among us knows me because of this man?"

A man named Rick Thurner from Buffalo, New York, rises. "I do, Lord." Another man, Curt Harmon, rises, "Me too, Lord."

After many hours a man named Rick Barron and his wife, Lea, finally rise, holding hands, and they both, in unison say, "Us too, Lord. Us too."

You blink your eyes and there she is. Your bride. Mary. Who's that walking not far behind her? Hmm. It's Bri and Brian, and Lauren and Taylor and their kids and their kids and their kids. Your family tree is alive and well. Its roots run deep and strong in Him.

§§§

Rick Thurner and Curt Harmon are friends you haven't met yet. But I have. Thank you, Gilbert, thank you.

You made a difference in my life. You loved me before I believed I was lovable.

I was put here on this earth to encourage you today, my friend. It's the very least I can do for you.

Faith is reaching into nowhere. Grabbing onto nothing. And holding on until it becomes something.

Let's hold on together . . . for him.

C'mon now. Gloooooooorrrrryyyy.

That'll cure what ails you now, Mister.

RB

Sometimes when we "water" others, they grow up and return the favor. Irrigate-ees become irrigate-ors. I just got doused by Rick . . . and . . . then my BlackBerry got doused by me. It was a moist morning.

5 SECONDS FROM ELVIS

By Rick Barron.
Used by permission.

*There was a drunk man in a speeding car, came up
    on my right
I touched the brakes, safe from him, as he swerved
    left that night
I checked the mirror, slowed myself, said son stay
    away from him
He's got a few too many, under his belt*

*But someone up ahead must've been twistin' their
    radio dial
'Cause sure enough, he caught their bumper and
    T-boned on the side
Now I asked myself should I stop or should I pass
    on by*

*But Lord knows people need a hand to hold, when
    the wreckage stops its slide*

*5 seconds from Elvis, that's where I'd turn out to be
5 seconds from Elvis as the passing car tore into me
You'd be surprised the kind of things you realize
When you're just, 5 seconds from Elvis*

*Now some they live the charmed life, and slip
    through the cracks
They race around us through the gate and never
    look back
I've seen surgery and sadness, there are purer
    things I've felt
I wouldn't change a card, in the hand that I've been
    dealt*

*'Cause 5 seconds from Elvis, is not such a bad place
    to be
5 seconds from Elvis taught me what you mean to
    me
And everything standing between the earth and the
    sky
Is just 5 seconds from Elvis*

*What does it mean to you, just one beat of your
    heart
I tell you what, it's everything,
It's where your life stops . . . and where your life
    starts*

*So if you're looking for a moral, some kind of
message from God
Some of his biggest lessons happen when life gets
hard
Ask yourself should you stop, or should you pass on
by
Think about how you would feel when the
wreckage stops its slide*

*5 seconds from Elvis, that's where we all love the
most
5 seconds from Elvis, is where life itself
unfolds
You'll be surprised by the next
year of your life
If you live 5 seconds from Elvis*

READY

Tookie called me while I was driving to a meeting today.

She said, "TERRY!" (It was a rather vociferous "Terry.") "TERRY, I've got some news for you . . . I am no longer an atheist."

Pause.

"And TERRY . . . I am no longer an agnostic."

Pause.

"So — what are you, Tookie?" I asked.

She answered with one word.

"Ready."

LAWN SIGN

I got a call a few months back from Paddle, my stogie-smokin'
Jackson Hole buddy. He said, "I gave your book to a friend
who is thinking about faith — the whole God-thing. Well, he
read it on the plane, and now he wants to have lunch with us
and talk."

The three of us met, and Tom started telling me his story.
Things weren't perfect, of course, they never are. He had some
health issues, life issues, but overall his life was almost story-
bookish. Successful businessman running out of rungs on his
ladder, influential, well-known, clout, great family, great life,
exploring candidacy for governor — number 10 with a bullet.

"So why are we here, Governor?" I asked with a smile.

"Here's the deal," Tom said. "I've planned my whole life.
I've scripted it, and so far it's tracking pretty close to script."
He paused. "But what if this God you talk about in your
book . . . well, what if my plan isn't his plan? What if he's
thinking something totally different? And if so, what if I don't
like his plan?

"You know what I'd like?" he continued. "I'd like to wake
up some morning and look out my front window and see a

lawn sign that God planted there overnight — a sign that says, 'Here's who you are, here's what I want you to do, and here's how I want you to do it.' If he would just do something like that, then I could check it out, and I'd know it was from him. Then I'd have something to work with, something to consider.

"I'd really like a sign," he concluded.

We talked for a while and then abruptly, in his typically unorthodox sort of directness, Paddle says, "Let's go guys, I want to take you on a field trip." Tom and I looked at each other. Paddle stood up and we followed, piling into his truck.

"Where are we going?"

"You'll see." He had that suspicious grin on his face. Made us nervous.

A few miles later we pulled into the parking lot of Paddle's church. I could see Tom's eyes. He was thinking, *Oh boy, what is this? Some sort of spiritual intervention thing?*

Paddle wouldn't say anything; we just followed him in. We walked down the center aisle of the sanctuary. He sat down in the front row. We sat.

He took a breath, then said, "Tom, you talk about wanting a sign. You've been looking for that sign your whole life. You've been hoping for that sign, but yet hoping against it, because you are in complete control of your life. You've planned it, you are living it. It's yours. It's what you have always wanted."

He continued, "You *say* you want a sign, but I'm not so sure you do. But . . . if you truly want one, well, you have one." Paddle's eyes looked up toward the front of the church. His eyes traced the huge cross hanging on the front wall. Then he said, "There's your sign. That's all the sign you need."

It was quiet for a minute. Then Paddle, with a calm

boldness said, "I think you need to step up there, kneel down, and say, 'that's the sign I'll follow, that's the direction for my life, that's all I need to know about how to live.' "

Tom walked up and knelt down. We went with him. He prayed.

God showed Tom a sign that day, but we, Paddle and I, got to help pound that sign into Tom's lawn. I planted one post by writing a book that describes the beauty of the sign. Paddle planted the other post by acting on a nudging, taking us on an unlikely field trip. And the rest was God's deal. Now Tom's life is God's deal. Tom is one more person who will help plant signs in the front lawns of others.

Being the Surprise is a trip, a daily field trip to only-*God*-knows-where. And he's the only one who needs to know. He is all the sign we need.

NOSE FOR GARBAGE

Our Springer Spaniel has a nose for garbage. I came home tonight only to find she had clawed open the garbage drawer in our kitchen, dragged out the bag, rummaged through the contents, and scattered it around the main floor of our house. The garbage contained a few of her favorites — paper towels that had been used to soak up the excess grease from this morning's bacon. Mmm. Who wouldn't want to snarf that?

This isn't the first time Bailey's done this. In fact, it's not the twentieth time. This dog could open a hermetically-sealed, titanium-encased missile silo if it had a scant scent of bacon grease wafting out.

I know how she works. When I leave the house, she gives me about a minute, then cases out all the wastebaskets, looking for the latest, greatest gunk.

Last night I yelled at her when I got home. I told her what a bad dog she was. I think she believed me too, because she could barely lift her nose from the floor two hours post-scolding. The only looks she gave me were out of the extreme corners of her eyes, and those were brief, fleeting glances. Eye contact was not her thing last night.

Later in the evening I took my delinquent dog for her nightly walk. She seemed happy to be walking *ahead* of me, where she wouldn't have to look *at* me. I stopped along our walk and looked up into the night sky. A gazillion stars were just hanging there. Vast. The infinity of the depth of space seemed more apparent to me than ever before. I imagined the universe as the galactic household of God — eight billion bedrooms, six trillion baths, and an 843,562-car garage . . . and me as his dog.

And as if that little skewering of self-identity wasn't bizarre enough, I then had an epiphany:

Even *God's* dog has a nose for garbage.

Yup, that's me we're talking about. When God leaves the house (my perception, not reality), I give him about a minute before my quest for trash gets the green light. Sniff, sniff, sin, sin.

Bailey is what she is. She's a dog. I know she's not the brightest creature, and her nose pretty much tells her brain what to do.

Sadly, me too.

So when I spread my trash around Ursa Major, why doesn't God yell at me, "Bad human!" Maybe even kick me once in a while. Why does he keep looking at me and empathizing, "I know you're human. I know your eyes tell your brain what to do." I half expect him to clip me onto a leash or at least send me outside to an invisibly-fenced-in planet. I expect some sort of confinement that will force me to live inside his *Behavioral Modification for Humans* rulebook.

But the leash never clicks on. The invisible fence doesn't exist. God doesn't curtail my eyes, my nose, my hands, my feet . . . *nada*. In fact, my will remains totally intact. I still roam freely with the same capacity and penchant to scrounge for garbage.

Why doesn't God exert at least minimal control over me? I do it to Bailey, and frankly, it makes me feel a bit better when I do.

I guess God doesn't see or treat me like a dog. I am one — I know it, he knows it — but still he treats me as if I'm something special. He doesn't leash me, he loves me. The only confinement I feel is that of an embrace. He doesn't hit, he holds.

True love doesn't demand. It models. There is no reciprocation rule. That kind of love can only be given, not taken.

God gave his love to me. He gave it completely, fully, in one fell swoop. In one act, he said, "I love you — I choose you." He sacrificed, proposed, wedded, and committed himself to me for eternity. And he did all this while I had my nose in the garbage — unleashed. What's more he *knew* I had my nose in the garbage while he was doing it all.

"But God put his love on the line for us by offering his Son in sacrificial death while we were of no use whatever to him" (Romans 5:8).

Wouldn't you think he would have hesitated? Wouldn't you think he would have gone, "Hey-hey-hey, see what I'm doing here? This is for you . . . you garbage-scrounging, dirt-nosed Spaniel."

As I stepped into the house with Bailey tonight, I patted

her on the head. She nuzzled my hand and all was forgiven. A minute later she was sleeping.

That's another thing I need to learn from her: how to receive love and forgiveness and forget everything in the past. She probably can't even remember I was mad or that she scrounged through the garbage. Clean slate, as if no garbage had ever been sniffed, spilled, or scarfed.

When God forgives me I need to lose my short-term memory and move on.

Knowing I'm loved and forgiven is likely to make me sniff a little less, scrounge a little less, live in the garbage a little less. Leashing my will could never change my desire; it would only restrict my capacity to act on that desire. God is less interested in my actions than in my heart. He wants my heart to *choose* my actions. He wants those choices to align with his heart *because* of my awareness of his great love and acceptance for me, whether I fall in line or not.

I'm developing a nose for better things. I want to be a friend to the one who is truly man's best friend. I want to please the one who gives me the *freedom* to please him. I want to obey the one who refuses to confine me to obedience. I want to be a best friend to the one who says, "Good human!" even when my goodness is terribly inhumane. I want to live distant from the garbage because *he can't go there with me.*

Knowing I'm loved, and unleashed, is what pulls me in that direction.

33

DON'T LOVE YOUR NEIGHBOR AS YOURSELF

Jesus said, "Love your neighbor as yourself."[5]
I used to think the problem with the world was that hardly anybody did this. I used to think that if everyone really started loving others as they loved themselves, the world would be unrecognizable, heaven-like.

I don't believe that anymore. In fact, I believe almost the opposite. Here's why.

The problem with the world is that most of us *do* love our neighbors as ourselves, in the same *way* we love ourselves. The catch? We don't love ourselves. We don't even like ourselves all that much. Our concept of self-love is messed up.

We don't like the way we look. We don't like our talents. We're not so crazy about our personalities. We're not as smart as we'd like to be. We look at the red carpet crowd and wish we were living their lives. We often feel that we have under-achieved, and because of that we don't feel particularly good

DON'T LOVE YOUR NEIGHBOR AS YOURSELF

about ourselves. Our self-esteem is shaky. It's not so much that we feel like failures, but we certainly don't feel like poster kids for success.

Then we take our battered self-image and assume God sees us the same way . . . as underachieving, unattractive, unwanted, unworthy, and unlovable pesky little peons who are more hassle than we are worth.

Not knowing any better, we turn around and love our neighbors exactly as we love ourselves. See the problem?

Loving our neighbors as ourselves will only work if we actually love ourselves in a proper, healthy sort of way — only if we see ourselves through God's eyes as worthy, wanted, and unconditionally accepted. Loved.

34

"DO I LOOK FAT?"

Do you ever sit down in front of the computer and scan blogs? I do. Not often, but every once in a while I give my eyes a chance to flip through the scratchings of Internet authors raging, ranting, and rambling about what life is like to be them. Cheap entertainment. Today one caught my eye. Here's an excerpt from that blog.

> The other night, I asked The Suitor the question no man likes to answer: "Do I look fat?" Instead of rolling his eyes, he replied, "You really want me to answer that?" I nodded a yes. "Fine, then I really need to get a good look." . . .
>
> "Hmm," he said with his finger on his chin. "Fat? Huh?" I held my breath, terrified he might say, "Yeah, you could stand to lose a good 15." Instead, he replied, "Stephanie, you are so hot. Don't you realize, I don't see you as fat or skinny? You are the love of my life. I see you as absolutely beautiful. You have to remember I don't see you like you see you. Do

you really want me to look at you as just fat or skinny?"

"No," I said in a small voice. Cause I already know I can stand to lose a good 15.

"Good, because you'd be doing us both a disservice. Just let me love you."[6]

When I was reading this blog, here's what I heard:

The other night I asked God the question he hates to answer: "Do I look, uh, good?" Instead of rolling his eyes, he replied, "You really want me to answer that?" I nodded. "Fine, but then I really need to get a good look."

"Hmm," he said with his finger on his chin. "Good? Huh?" I held my breath, terrified he might say, "Yeah, you could stand to clean your act up a good 15%." Instead, he replied, "Terry, you are so loved. Don't you realize I don't see you as good or bad? You are the love of my life. I see you as absolutely beautiful. You have to remember I don't see you like you see yourself. Do you really want me to look at you as simply good or bad?"

"No," I said in a small voice. Cause I already know I'm messed up.

"Good, because you'd be doing us both a disservice. Just let me love you."

When this is our picture of God, trust isn't such a reach. This picture of God makes me want to fold my life and plans and the moments of my days into his. It's easy for me to believe that such a God will not only surprise me with what's best and with what I need, but that he will place me in situations to Be the Surprise for others in ways that I can only dream about.

When this is our picture of God, we won't obsess about whether each move we make will make us look good. We know we already look good to God.

When this is our picture of God, we won't need to strive, prove, measure, gauge, compete, compare, or perpetually wonder if we are enough.

"Just let me love you."

FEBRUARY FIRE

A Parable

My fire went out in November. It's not that I ran out of wood or paper, I just ran out of — well, fire. I still had everything I needed to make a fire — all the ingredients — but something was missing, the something that makes heat, warmth. I couldn't find it and didn't even know where to look for it.

When I think about it now, my fires had never been much to brag about. It's not that they didn't look "fire-ish," but they always had a showroom quality to them . . . more pizzazz than essence. They had sparkle to burn, but no blaze to warm. They cast shadows, but couldn't throw heat.

At first I was okay without heat, as long as the fire burned big and bright. If the fire was flashy enough I could almost talk myself into feeling the warmth. But gradually, even the imagined heat escaped up the chimney. That's when the cold became real, when the chill entered my home. One day I sat down in front of my fire and saw it for what it was . . . artificial, hollow. And I was cold.

For the next month I did everything in my power to coax my hearth to life. I went through boxes of matches, stacks of papers. I created sparks without fire, flames without heat. I tried burning a lot of different things that made some pretty hot claims, but they all left me cold.

In the evening I would go for walks, long walks. My favorite walk took me by the Wellington Mansion. It was the original house in Bakersville. The centerpiece of our little town. It was over a mile from my house, but worth every step. The place glowed, practically radiated heat. Mr. Wellington had fire, lots of it. I think I counted twelve chimneys and half of them had a fire at all times.

For weeks I walked slowly by the house, watching the smoke curl from the chimney tops. I walked downwind so I could smell the fire. I climbed snow banks so I could look in the windows and see the firelight flickering against the walls. It was a study in light. I imagined the warmth on my skin, my face.

Every day I fought the urge to approach the front door, ring the bell, and invite myself in. I had heard that Mr. Wellington was a kindly old gentleman, generous with strangers, but I'd never met him personally. I couldn't just waltz up to his door and expect him to drop everything and give me a tour. It seemed so presumptuous.

One night, I told myself I'd just walk up to the door. I wouldn't ring the bell, I'd just get close. I climbed the last four steps, hands in my pockets, trying to look casual, inconspicuous. In front of the door was a big Welcome mat. On the wall was an engraved bronze plaque that said, "Make Yourself at Home." Maybe it was the plaque, maybe it was the wind, but I involuntarily reached for the bell and pushed it.

When no one answered I was almost relieved. I noticed the inner door was slightly ajar, an inch or so. I knocked, surprisingly hard. Still nothing. Feeling very cold and having spent so much courage just getting to this point, I pulled the storm door open a foot and yelled, "Hello. Anybody home?" No response. All I could hear was the crackling of the fire in the next room. I stepped just inside the door, wondering where this dose of courage had come from. "Excuse me. Um, I was just wondering if, uh, if it would be all right with you if I came in and just, um, stood by your fire? Just for a minute or so?" Still nothing. "Anyone?"

I started to feel ill at ease, not to mention uninvited, and turned to leave. Just then a loud snap from the fire reminded me of my chill. I turned back and looked around the foyer. Above me hung a beautiful chandelier with a thousand glowing crystalline pendants. A wide arcing staircase of maple and cherry lay straight ahead of me. It ascended counterclockwise to a balcony lined with heavily-framed landscape paintings. The walls were a mix of mahogany trim and deep burgundy paint.

The fire snapped again. I made a mental calculation . . . *if I take two considerable steps straight ahead, I should be able to look into the living room and see the fire. Why not,* I thought, *I'm this far in.* I took those two giant steps and turned to face the room. I felt the warm glow on my face before I had even finished the turn.

The fire captured me. I had an instantaneous feeling of connection with something that had been missing, absent, lost. I felt a surge of emotion — at first I thought it was fear — but I knew it was more than just that. Not sure how to handle this avalanche of feelings, I turned and ran out the door.

I was still warm when I arrived home. I made a cup of hot tea and sat down in my big, soft chair in the living room. I tried to picture what else had been in that room with the fire, but I realized I hadn't even looked at anything else. I had a vivid mental picture of the entryway, but the living room? Nothing. The fire had so consumed me that its presence was my only memory — nothing else had even registered.

As I sat in my chair, reliving the evening, something caught my attention. I thought I smelled something. Smoke. I jumped up and started checking around the house. Was something burning? I looked everywhere, upstairs and down . . . nothing. I came back to the living room. There it was again, a faint smell of smoke. I figured it had to be coming from one of the neighbor's houses and let it go at that. I closed my eyes, picturing Mr. Wellington's fire, and fell fast asleep.

The next night I returned to the Wellington Mansion. Chunky snowflakes were falling through the evergreens in front of the house, and light was sifting through the windows, dancing on the floating, white crystals. The warm pull was irresistible. Without hesitation, I walked up to the door and rang the bell.

Again there was no answer. I noticed the stately wooden door was even further ajar tonight; it was practically swung open. A handwritten note was attached to the plaque. In graceful penmanship it simply said, "Please, come on in. Make yourself completely at home."

So, he saw me last night. Why hadn't he come down, said, "Hi"? Had he been watching me the whole time? I stepped inside the door.

"Hello? Mr. Wellington?" As I waited for a response, I kicked the snow off my shoes. "You have a beautiful place here." I took another step in. "Would you mind if I just warmed myself by your fire for a minute or two again? I won't be long." The only sound was the crackling of the fire. I followed it into the living room.

It was everything I had remembered. Every inch of the hearth flashed with flames. Several good-sized logs lay on a gleaming bed of coals. The logs looked as if they had been freshly laid on the fire. Had Mr. Wellington seen me coming? Had he refreshed the fire, just for me?

I walked closer to the fire this time, halfway across the living room. The warmth saturated me immediately. I felt a droplet of water land on my nose as the fire melted the snow on my hair.

I reached my hands toward the fire, receiving its warmth, pulling it toward me. My muscles relaxed. My breathing slowed. The heat almost seemed to erase the months I'd spent without fire. The flames touched me in a healing way, in places I never knew needed healing. As I left I yelled from the entryway, "Thanks, Mr. Wellington. Thanks for sharing your fire."

As soon as I opened the front door of my house I knew something was different. The smell of smoke was much stronger than it had been the previous night. I put my sleeve up to my nose, thinking maybe my clothes had taken on the smell from Mr. Wellington's fire, but I knew — I knew that wasn't it. As I rounded the kitchen and headed for the living room, I saw the glow. The room was bathed in a faint amber tint. Subtle, but certain. I peeked around the corner toward the fireplace. I couldn't believe what I saw. It was beautiful. There was no fire, but the hearth was covered with embers, a bed of red-hot coals. The room had a warmth it hadn't enjoyed for months. My home was coming back to life.

It didn't make any sense, this rekindling, but yet it seemed completely natural. Back in November I had ignited all kinds of things on my own and never produced a heat I could feel. This new beginning felt real.

The next evening I was even more eager to pay my nightly visit to the mansion. Things were turning around for me and, in large part, it seemed due to my new acquaintance with Mr. Wellington and his fire.

As I skipped up the walk I noticed another note hanging on the door. It said, "I enjoyed your visit last night. Please feel free to stay as long as you like, till you're warm. Try out my chair. I moved it in front of the fire just for you."

I did. This was the closest yet I had been to the fire. The chair had been placed squarely in front of the hearth. I fell into it, surprised how well it fit me . . . like it had been custom-built for me. I took off my shoes and stretched my legs toward the fire. I was sitting in a stranger's house, and yet I was completely comfortable, completely at home.

I stared into the fire for hours that night, mesmerized by the blue, red, and yellow flames. They seemed to talk to me, telling me where I'd been and where I was going. They showed me who I was and who I could be. I saw ashes of failure and sparks of hope. The chimney carried the sparks heavenward and sprinkled them across the night sky. I had a sense that I had been freed by the fire; the darkness lifted, the chill released. I snuggled down into the leather chair and fell asleep under a peaceful blanket of warm.

The sun was just beginning to flirt with the horizon when I woke up. I was toasty, my cheeks rosy red. I sprang from the chair with an excitement I hadn't had in . . . well, ever. I threw on my shoes and ran out the door. Halfway down the walk I skidded to a stop, wheeled, and ran back inside. With a lilt in my voice I said, "I still haven't stayed as long as I'd like, but I'm getting there. Thanks, Mr. Wellington. See you tonight."

As I started jogging toward home, my mind jumped from his fireplace to mine. *Will my coals be even brighter, hotter?* I notched it up a few miles per hour. As I ran down the middle of the road, skipping over the long shadows of dawn, I felt the steam coming off my heat-saturated body. *Will the glow still be there?* Anticipation coaxed me into a full-out sprint. *Did I dare to wish for fire?* I practically flew around the last corner, squinting down to the end of the block. I pulled up abruptly and stood, staring in the middle of the street.

Through the steamy mist of my own frozen breath I gazed toward my house. My knees gave a quiver as I realized that it was *my* house that was aglow, *my* windows that were ablaze, and *my* chimney that was puffing like an industrial smoke stack.

I did the last hundred yards in ten-flat. I threw open the door and skittered across the hardwood floor, sliding the last few steps into the living room. Before I could even look, the snap-crackling told the story. It was an inferno, the biggest fire my hearth had ever seen; not just sparkle and flash, but sizzle and fizz. It was throwing strikes of pure heat. It was real, the fire was real. The snap was familiar, the warmth reminiscent of a fire I had come to know. Mr. Wellington's fire had come home to my home.

I spent the day in a dreamland. I had never spent an entire day barefoot and warm, in winter. I danced around in a T-shirt. I ate frozen yogurt and drank iced tea. My house was so hot, I even left my front door cracked open.

I had heat to spare.

At about seven o'clock that night I grabbed my coat and gloves and headed for the front door. Even though I had my own fire now, I was still drawn to Mr. Wellington's . . . maybe even more so *because* I had my own fire. It's hard to explain.

As I pushed open the front door, I ran head-first into a woman standing on my steps. I grabbed her arm just in time to keep her from falling off the steps into my shrubs.

"Oh, oh, I'm sorry," I said. "I didn't see you there. Are you okay?"

She was even more startled than me. Flustered and confused . . . and embarrassed. "You must think I'm a snoop. I'm not, really, I'm just . . ."

"No, that's okay. You just startled me," I said, trying to downplay the situation. Whoever this woman was, we were getting off to an awkward start.

Finally, I looked at her, in the eyes. She was middle-aged, with eyes that looked sad. She was looking down at her feet when she decided to speak. "I'm really sorry, but I was just, well . . . I'll, I'll come back later . . . you're leaving, so I'll just come back . . ." She trailed off as she turned to leave.

"No," I said. "I'm in no huge rush. What can I do for you, Miss . . . ?"

"Jen, Jennifer. I live two doors down. Right over there." She pointed.

"Hi Jennifer. I thought you looked familiar." Then I added,

"You look . . . cold. How long have you been out here?"

She paused. "A while."

It seemed as if she was trying to figure out what to say. She finally found some momentum. "You'll probably think I'm nuts, but I've been looking at your house all day. Your windows — they're glowing. I noticed your chimney — it's busy." We both smiled. "Well, you've obviously got a fire in there and, well, uh, my fire went out a while back, and, I was just wondering if, if I could . . ."

". . . come in and stand by my fire?" I finished her question for her. She looked like she was caught between a smile and tears.

"I've got an even better idea," I said. "Wanna see the best, most beautiful fire in the world?" I didn't wait for her answer, I just started tugging her down the street. As she bounced along beside me I told her my story, which I suspected would soon be her story.

Anyhow, that's how I found fire . . . for real. I haven't figured it all out yet, but one thing I do know . . . I was cold but now I'm warm. It's February, and I've got a new fire burning in my home.

One thing I do know. I was blind but now I see!
John 9:25, NIV

36

STAND BY YOUR FIRE

Song lyrics by John Olson & Terry Esau

Well I'm here at your door like some poor relation
I seem to be looking for some quick salvation
But I don't really have any expectations
Just let me stand by your fire

Oh I know you're the one that I disowned
But my fortune has fallen, the sweet bird has flown
And I got me a shiver running straight to the bone
Just let me stand by your fire

(Chorus)
Let me stand by your fire until you melt me
Let me feel your tender love so warm
Oh my heart is aching and my soul is tired
Just let me stand by your fire

Oh the glow of your light that now
    surrounds me
Is the day to the night that your
    fire found me
And I'm free from the chill that so
    long had bound me
Now that I stand by your fire

(Chorus)
Let me stand by your fire until you melt me
Let me feel your tender love so warm
Oh my heart is aching and my soul is tired
Just let me stand by your fire

37

COFFEE MONEY

"Today I sign the papers to surrender my seven million dollar company. At two o'clock this afternoon, in my attorney's office, it will all be gone — everything I've spent my life on, everything I've worked for."

Tyler's eyes were filled with tears as he told me his story.

Last Sunday he had sent me an e-mail saying he had picked up the last copy of my book *Surprise Me* at the Retro Roast Coffee Shop in Loretto. He had read it and was wondering if I would be willing to sit down with him and talk. He said his life was falling apart and that he could really use a friend.

I sent an e-mail back, saying that I would meet him at Retro on Tuesday morning at nine.

As we sat down, Tyler laid out the story of the collapse of his printing business. All the franchises, gone. All the potential, gone. Lawsuits and choices had pulled him under. I could hear the regrets choke him as he spelled them out, one by one. By 2 p.m. the regrets would no longer matter; it would be over.

Even though I could tell this guy was in great shape, his shoulders were sagging under the weight of fear and "what's next?" Hope had vacated his eyes; I could see worry crowding in around the corners. He wasn't shaking, but he had an unsteadiness as he spoke, as if he was taking careful verbal steps to keep from falling.

He told me his self-confidence was about as low as it could get, and I could tell he didn't have a plan in place for rebuilding it.

"When I realized this was all crashing down," he said, "I started going to that little Catholic church across the street. Almost every morning I sit there from eight to nine, alone in a pew, sometimes crying." He talked of wrestling with faith and God, wondering if he had brought this on himself or if God was punishing him. Was God trying to tell him something, or had he just made errors, business errors, with natural consequences?

He told me that his house was going on the market the next day. A one-and-a-half million dollar house, their dream home — liquidated. Six months earlier he had rewarded himself for reaching a new benchmark in his business by buying a Mercedes SL convertible. He told me what it felt like to tape the For Sale signs in the windows and park it on the streets of downtown Wayzata. Afterward he'd sat on a park bench with his head in his hands, wondering how it had come to this.

We talked for two-and-a-half hours that morning. I tried to encourage him, to prop hope back up for him. I told him that I cared about him and I knew God did too. I told him that I wanted to be his friend.

I asked him how his wife, Marissa, was doing. Tyler told me she could really use a friend, someone to talk to. She'd become more and more accustomed to the perks of wealth on the way up, and now, on the way down, she was holding on for dear life as the things she loved were slipping through her fingers.

I told Tyler that my wife was a great listener, and if he wanted, we could both come over that evening around nine. He said he'd like that, and as I left the coffee shop, I said, "We'll see you guys tonight at nine . . . hang in there."

As I was driving away, a thought popped into my head. *What if I were to call twenty of my friends, ask them to write Tyler a check for one hundred dollars, and show up at his house tonight at nine-thirty and hand him the check.* (FYI: This is not a typical thought for me, nor one that I have ever acted on before.)

But I did—this time. I called twenty of my good friends, some of whom that hundred dollars was little more than pocket change and some who would need to radically alter their monthly budget to fit it in. I e-mailed them all with the address and directions to get there.

Mary got home from work around six and did a quick turnaround so we could meet some friends for dinner at seven. As we drove to the restaurant, I started telling her about my interesting day and the unorthodox plan for later that evening. As I was telling her, I remembered another detail about that morning. When I had arrived at Retro, I had parked across the street because the parking lot was full. As I got out of my car, I saw three guys walking down the street toward Retro. One guy glanced over at me and said, "Hi, Terry." I didn't recognize him but walked up to see who it was. He introduced himself as Paul and said he had heard me launch the Surprise Me experiment at a church a while back and had read the book. He said he had enjoyed it and was inviting God into his days.

Tyler, who was walking from his car, had overheard Paul

say my name and came over and said, "You're Terry? I'm Tyler, the guy you're meeting with today." We all said hi and went into Retro.

Now, ten hours later, as Mary and I are driving to dinner, I said, "I wish I knew the last name of that Paul guy I met on the street this morning. It would be fun to invite him to the 9:30 deal at Tyler and Marissa's." But directory assistance isn't very helpful if all you've got is a first name. So I told Mary, "I'm going to call the coffee shop. They might know his last name since his office is across the street, plus he seemed like a regular."

I called Retro, but Heidi and Bill, the owners, were gone and nobody else knew who I was talking about. Oh well, I tried.

As Mary and I walked into Maynard's Grill in Excelsior, which is about thirty miles from Retro, I almost bumped into Paul. For the second time that day he said, "Hi, Terry." This time he cocked his head a bit as he said it, with a fancy-meeting-you-*again*-today look.

I told him I had spent the last ten minutes trying to track him down to invite him to tonight's deal. "What deal?" he asked. I briefly brought him up to speed on my discussion with Tyler, reminding him that he had met Tyler on the street that morning. He said, "I'll be there with a check, wouldn't miss it — 9:30 sharp."

Dinner was great. We told our friends, DeVon and Joanne, about the day's events and the meeting yet to come. Before we left, they handed us an envelope of cash they had found in a drawer, where it had been tucked away for twelve years. They had been planning on using it to help pay for the dinner but asked us to give it to Tyler and Marissa.

Mary and I arrived at their house with a certain measure of trepidation. What was this conversation going to be like? How would they react to a group of strangers bearing gifts? What if the strangers bearing gifts were no-shows? What if the "wise men" were too busy tonight to ride their camels to the far side of Orono — no gold, frankincense, or myrrh?

As we walked between the pillars up to the front door, it made me think of a phrase my friend Tookie uses when seeing a house that is somewhere beyond stunning, but just short of ostentatious . . . she refers to it as a Starter Castle. I thought, *I've just asked some dear friends, some of whom are struggling financially, to walk up to this Starter Castle and cheerfully give the resident king and queen one hundred of their hard-earned dollars. This is crazy!*

Crazy? Yes. But also the right thing to do. I knew it. Everything about this scene seemed upside-down and backward, which made me suspect, even more so, that God was in it.

The first few minutes were a bit awkward. Nobody likes to undress financially in front of strangers. We humans aren't fond of staying centerstage when we've totally forgotten our lines. However, Tyler and Marissa weren't running or hiding. They were broken, but standing still in humility, owning their brokenness, maybe admitting for the first time in their lives that they couldn't dig or buy their way out of this hole.

Tyler was telling me that his nature as an introvert and his focus on work had hindered them from having significant friendships. That's when the doorbell rang. As I walked him to the door, I let him in on the news that we had invited a few of our friends to come over and help if they could.

We opened the front door to a crowd of beautiful angels encircling the doorway, eager to bless these strangers. I couldn't see the wings — it was too dark — but I think I heard them.

Tyler invited this group of people he had never laid eyes on into his living room. As they came in, one by one, they placed a check or hundred-dollar bill in his shaking hand. Tears were streaming down Tyler's face. Marissa stood in disbelief as the parade of generosity continued.

Bill and Heidi, the owners of Retro were there. Didn't they know we had only ordered a couple of smoothies that morning? That's a negative profit ratio.

Paddle was there. HipWaders was there. Some of my cycling buddies were there. Our small-group friends were represented.

Paul, the "Hi, Terry" Paul, was there. And he brought Gunner, a business associate from California with him. Strangers had invited other strangers.

I've never been so proud of my friends as I was in that moment. I've never been so humbled to have the kind of friends who wear wings unaware. Many of them never asked me a single detail about Tyler's situation. They never said, "What's his story? Is he legit? Are we being taken?" Nothing like that. They thanked *me* for honoring them with the invitation. Unbelievable.

We stood in a circle for a half hour that night. People shared about times in their lives when things had collapsed and told of how they had gotten through it. They painted pictures of hope, a future that could and would walk again. They pointed to a distant light at the end of a dark tunnel. They talked of grace and healing.

Gary wrapped up our circle time with this. "I know you guys lost seven million today, and that hurts. I understand that. A year ago I lost my wife, and I'd give seven *billion* dollars right now for five minutes with Cheryl . . . you still have each other. You haven't lost everything. Tyler, you have Marissa. Marissa, you have Tyler. You've got God. You'll get through this, you'll make it."

We closed with a prayer and hugs as the group filtered out.

When Mary and I arrived home, there was an envelope on our kitchen table with almost six hundred dollars in it from people who couldn't make it to the house. The next morning Garlington Northern showed up at their house with a check. People e-mailed me, asking for Tyler and Marissa's mailing address. Checks are still coming in. From perfect strangers.

The next morning I got a call from Gary. With a laugh he said, "Hey, Terry, thanks for inviting me to church last night!" It was. My friends were the church, mobilized and selfless.

Tyler told me later, "I have never accepted charity before . . . I have never borrowed from anyone. Well, once, my mom begged my dad to give me ten dollars while I was in college. But that is the only money I have ever accepted from anyone in my life, ever."

Until now.

Opening his hand and holding it there while person after person placed one hundred dollars in his palm was one of the hardest things he had ever done. But I think it marked a

turning point in his life.

We accept charity only when we are in a position of need, of insufficiency. A position that says, "I'm not making it here; I need your help." Until we can see our own need, we'll never accept help.

Until we *know* we're not enough, we'll never accept grace.

And until we accept grace, we'll never *be* enough.

Tyler and Marissa may have had to lose it all in order to keep from "losing it all." Running out of rope may have been the only thing to keep them from falling. They lost a lot this week, but I'm not so sure they didn't find more.

INTERRUPTING COW

I was getting my hair cut last week and Nina, my stylist, said, "Stephanie told me this joke. She's only six, and she made it up.

> "Knock, knock.
> Who's there?
> Interrupting cow.
> Interrupting cow, wh —
> MOO!!"

Stephanie's joke reminds me of something Henri Nouwen said in his later years: "My whole life I have been complaining that my work was constantly interrupted, until I discovered the interruptions *were* my work."[7] Mark Buchanan says we need to "become hospitable to interruption."[8]

If my home has a real fire, throwing real heat, sooner or later someone will show up on my front steps wanting to be warmed. When that interruption happens, I want to be hospitable to it.

I want to experience the Fire myself, and then I want to grab the hands of cold people and bring them to the Fire, to grow the "G," to be the domestique, to be Wilma to the world. To spontaneously live and love with a faith that's real. Continually receiving — continually giving.

Here's my spin on Stephanie's joke.

> Knock, knock.
> Who's there?
> Interrupting God.
> Interrupting God who?
> I'm the God who wants to interrupt the world *with* you . . . to love the world *with* you, *through* you. I want you to interrupt your neighbors with my love, your kids, your friends, your spouse, your co-workers, the guy next to you in line at Starbucks . . . the world. This is how I want the two of us to spend our days.
> Even as I have surprised you, now go and . . . Be the Surprise.

NOTES

1. In case you're wondering, this is *not* God as a genie in a bottle. I'm not suggesting that God will pop out of his lamp and grant us three wishes if we pray "Surprise me, God" frequently and fervently enough. I'm asking for what *God* wants to bring into my life.
2. Kyriacos C. Markides, *The Mountain of Silence* (Image Publishing, 2002), 87.
3. Kyle Lake, *Understanding God's Will* (Orlando, FL: Relevant Books, 2004), 67.
4. Used with permission.
5. Matthew 22:39, NIV.
6. From a blog by Stephanie Klein (http://stephanieklein .blogs.com/greek_tragedy/2005/11/index.html).

   (The publisher wishes to warn readers that some things on this site may be offensive. The views expressed on this site are solely those of Ms. Klein and don't necessarily represent the views of NavPress.)
7. Mark Buchanan, "Schedule, Interrupted: Discovering God's Time-management," *Christianity Today*, Feb. 2006, Volume 50, No. 2, 43.

8. Mark Buchanan, "Schedule, Interrupted: Discovering God's Time-management," *Christainity Today*, Feb. 2006, Volume 50, No. 2.

TERRY ESAU

Speaker, Author, Musician

From small-town punk, playing in a basement band (cellar-dwelling cousin of the garage band) with his Fender amp cranked to eleven — stomping on his wah-fuzz pedal — to becoming the Jingle King of Minneapolis, Terry has written and produced thousands of pieces of music for TV commercials — from Target to McDonalds, Pepsi to Perkins, Harleys to Hondas, and Golden Grahams to Billy Graham. He climbed the creative corporate ladder only to find disenchantment once there.

That's when he got proactive. He wrote a book called *Blue Collar God/White Collar God*. He started telling stories about the one product that he knew could *change* people's lives — a relationship with God. He knew because it changed his life.

Now he's taking this story on the road. The Surprise Me Experiment, based on his book, *Surprise Me*, is getting rolled out in churches, college campuses, and groups of every kind across America. *Be the Surprise* continues that movement with the next step in the *Experiments of Spontaneous Faith*. Terry spends much of his time traveling and speaking to audiences, encouraging this life of adventure and surprise.

Terry and his wife, Mary, have three daughters, one son-in-law, and a disobedient dog. They live in Minneapolis, Minnesota.

For more information and to find out how to bring these Experiments of Spontaneous Faith to your church, college, or group:

www.SurpriseMeGod.com

Nudge the World
P.O. Box 474
Minneapolis, MN 55356

Terry@SurpriseMeGod.com

952-476-2204

www.myspace.com/terryesau
www.100bucks.org

Break Out of the Ho-Hum Spiritual Life

Surprise Me

Terry Esau
ISBN-13: 978-1-57683-823-5
ISBN-10: 1-57683-823-4

"Surprise me, God." What if you started the next thirty days with this simple prayer? No agendas, no plans other than waiting on God with eager anticipation of what is about to happen next. *Surprise Me* invites you to approach your spiritual life with openness and an eye for the unexpected to discover God working the everyday moments in your life, from the spectacular to the mundane. Author Terry Esau illustrates why everyday surprises, when examined, reveal God's grace and calling that breathes new life into your faith journey.

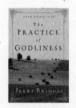

The Practice of Godliness

Jerry Bridges

ISBN-13: 978-0-89109-941-3
ISBN-10: 0-89109-941-7

What makes someone godly? Scripture tells us that God has given us "everything we need for life and godliness." But what makes a Christian godly? In *The Practice of Godliness*, Jerry Bridges examines what it means to grow in Christian character and helps us establish the foundation upon which that character is built.

Buck Naked Faith

Eric Sandras
ISBN-13: 978-1-57683-525-8
ISBN-10: 1-57683-525-1

Honest and gritty, Eric Sandras wants to encourage a generation of believers to drop the layers of make-believe that stunt our spiritual growth. In the process, he exposes the naked truth: We need to dress our lives with a real friendship with God and nothing else.

Visit your local Christian bookstore, call NavPress at
1-800-366-7788, or log on to www.navpress.com to purchase.
To locate a Christian bookstore near you, call 1-800-991-7747.